Formative Assessment
in Practice

Formative Assessment in Practice

A Process of Inquiry and Action

MARGARET HERITAGE

Harvard Education Press
Cambridge, Massachusetts

Assessment Accountability & Achievement | SERIES

Library of Congress Control Number 2012955423

Paperback ISBN 978-1-61250-551-0
Library Edition ISBN 978-1-61250-552-7

Published by Harvard Education Press,
an imprint of the Harvard Education Publishing Group

Harvard Education Press
8 Story Street
Cambridge, MA 02138

Cover Design: Joel Gendron
Cover Photo: © Hero/Corbis
The typefaces used in this book are Minion, Myriad Pro, and Myriad Condensed

Contents

Dualism's Dividends

Practitioners are different than academics. Practitioners make things work. Academics increase knowledge about how things work. *Educational* practitioners exude practicality—they want to know how to improve schooling today or, at the latest, tomorrow. *Educational* academics, in contrast, are immersed in scholarship—eagerly perusing peer-refereed journals as they report their findings to tiny cadres of similarly disposed scholars. Rarely does one encounter a writer who can deftly hop between the academic and practitioner sandboxes. Happily, Margaret Heritage can do so—and in this thought-provoking new book, she does so with style and grace.

Although in recent years Heritage has been engaged in the academic enterprise, based at the University of California, Los Angeles, much of her previous career has been patently practical. She was a classroom teacher for eight years, a school administrator for a dozen years, and an inspector in the United Kingdom for four years. When she writes about formative assessment, she has not forgotten from whence she came. In *Formative Assessment in Practice: A Process of Inquiry and Action*, she capitalizes fully on this dual persona as she tackles the formative assessment process from both a practical and a scholarly perspective.

Heritage kicks her book into gear by endorsing a "children's rights approach to assessment." This perspective, as readers will learn, underlies her entire conception of formative assessment; namely, not only why it works, but why truly responsible educators ought to employ it. Drawing on a series of international conventions, starting in 1924 and extending through the 1989 United Nations Convention on the Rights of the Child, Heritage explains that children's rights include access to learning, the chance to develop their full potential, and a voice in matters that affect their futures. She argues persuasively that a classroom culture that incorporates formative assessment, embraces personalized learning, and embodies a community of practice satisfies these rights.

Heritage's early advocacy of an assessment approach based on children's rights offers her readers a key insight about the way she regards the mission of formative assessment. Although most authorities agree that formative assessment allows both teachers and their students to use evidence of student learning to determine whether they need to make adjustments in the classroom, there is a distinctive difference between the way U.S. educators and their European counterparts regard the formative assessment process. If you were to ask American educators to describe what the chief function of formative assessment is, they would most likely tell you that it provides evidence that allows *teachers* to adjust their instructional procedures. If the same query were posed to a similar sample of European educators, you would most likely hear them say that it helps *students* decide whether they need to make adjustments in their approach to learning. In the United States, we stress the role of formative assessment in helping teachers optimize their instruction. In Europe, educators emphasize the role of formative assessment in assisting students to become more effective, autonomous learners.

Heritage deftly captures both of these perspectives in this exciting new book. She brings to her U.S. readers a set of student-focused insights not often presented in American writings about formative assessment. For instance, her recommendation that "personalized learning" become a key outcome of formative assessment will cause many U.S. educators to think twice about how formative assessment really ought to be used in the classroom. Personalized learning, as Heritage sees it, is aimed at fostering students' ability to learn independently via "interaction, intervention, stimulation, and collaboration." She argues that personalized learning can foster the dispositions, habits, attitudes, and identities allowing students to become lifelong learners. A conception of formative assessment focused on the promotion of personalized learning is vastly different from formative assessment characterized as teachers' merely using classroom tests to shape up their teaching.

In a particularly arresting chapter, Heritage describes the nature and nuances of a "community of practice" as a framework for any classroom committed to the formative assessment process. She points out that when individuals participate in a community of practice, the collective practices of the community are codetermined by its participants. Acting within a community of practice significantly shapes a student's identity as a learner, and this newly molded identity is then reflected in the behaviors and perceptions of other class members.

Moving from the conceptual to the practical, Heritage also discusses the range of evidence that teachers can gather about student learning, and the need to plan this evidence gathering well ahead of the actual assessment. Based on her own research, she also stresses the need for teachers to anticipate the responses students are apt to give and to consider suitable pedagogical moves to address those probable responses.

In a final, bravura chapter, Heritage joins forces with her colleague and friend E. Caroline Wylie to argue that the effective implementation of formative assessment—indeed, its very existence—is dependent on appropriate policy support. After considering a series of lessons learned from Australia, Canada, England, Finland, France, New Zealand, Norway, and Scotland, Heritage and Wylie identify policies that, if adopted, could enable the widespread implementation of formative assessment. Rarely are readers treated to such a clear and thoughtful analysis of the way so many nations are promoting formative assessment.

In metaphysics, epistemology, and theology, *dualism* refers to a conceptualization of reality based on two distinct, nonoverlapping categories. In this book, we see that Margaret Heritage has, to our benefit, overlapped up a storm. Her analysis of formative assessment reflects the real-world, what's-next thinking of a seasoned practitioner and, at the same time, the carefully documented, thoroughly researched approach of a full-fledged academic. Her readers are fortunate that she could not keep those two worlds apart.

—W. James Popham
Emeritus Professor of Education
University of California, Los Angeles

Introduction

No two children are the same. They come to learn in school from a range of backgrounds, cultures, and language groups, and they bring with them a set of diverse experiences. They learn in different ways and at different rates, and they have different motivations for learning and distinctive interests in its pursuit. A one-size-fits-all approach to learning does not accommodate the diversity of learners found in our classrooms. This diversity means that we need skilled teachers who, rather than standardizing learning for all, are able to respond to students as individuals. This involves shaping learning experiences on a daily basis in order to make appropriate demands on each student and ordering these experiences so that every successive element leads the student to realize desired learning goals. At the heart of responding to each student is individually sized learning. And assessment can pave the way to learning that is individually sized.

Assessment has two fundamental purposes. The first is to provide information on students' current levels of achievement to the present time. The second is to inform the future steps that teachers and students need to take to ensure that students make progress toward desired outcomes. In broad terms, assessments that provide information on students' current levels of achievement represent a *past-to-present* perspective of learning in the sense that they indicate what has been learned to date. Many goals of assessment require this past-to-present view of learning, for example, accountability, placement, and certification. By contrast, the goals of assessment in support of taking future steps in learning require a *present-to-future* perspective, in which the concern is not solely with the actual level of performance, but with anticipating future possibilities.[1] The contrast between these two perspectives is nicely captured by Frederick Erickson when he observed that, in addition to looking "upstream at what has been learned, assessment needs to look downstream at what *can be learned*."[2]

This book is about the second purpose of assessment—anticipating future possibilities for each student and planning individually sized learning opportunities so as to realize those possibilities. While the book is concerned with assessment as the linchpin to continuously advance learning for all students, it is not about tests or testing. Rather, the book presents an account of formative assessment, a set of practices that have been shown to improve learning for all students.

In their landmark review of formative assessment, building on prior reviews, Paul Black and Dylan Wiliam proposed that effective formative assessment involves:

- Teachers making adjustments to teaching and learning in response to assessment evidence;
- Students receiving feedback about their learning with advice on what they can do to improve; and
- Students' participation in the process through self-assessment.[3]

Throughout this book, we will consider each one of these attributes of formative assessment in detail, and examine how formative assessment can become deeply embedded in all aspects of teaching and learning so that teachers can effectively advance the learning of each one of their diverse students.

Our consideration of formative assessment will be framed by the perspective of children's rights. Access to learning, irrespective of the child's own context, is an important aspect of children's rights, and these rights embrace the practice of assessment.

A CHILDREN'S RIGHTS APPROACH TO ASSESSMENT

A series of international conventions, beginning with the Geneva Declaration of the Rights of the Child in 1924, have affirmed and reaffirmed the rights of children (every human being under the age of 18) to "particular care." Recognized in the Universal Declaration of Human Rights in 1948, the most recent 1989 United

Nations Convention on the Rights of the Child (CRC) includes a specific provision on education as a child's right, as well as the right that children will not be discriminated against. Among its provisions, Article 29 of the CRC defines a child's right to education as involving "the development of the child's personality, talents and mental and physical abilities to [his or her] fullest potential" and "the preparation of the child for a responsible life in a free society."[4] Two additional principles of the CRC emphasize that 1) in all decisions made about children, their best interests must be a primary concern; and 2) children have a right to have their views given "due weight" in all matters affecting them.[5]

Although assessment is not explicitly mentioned in the CRC, the fact that assessment is a significant part of the fabric of education in many countries of the world has led scholars to consider children's rights in this context. In a powerful discussion on the rights of the child in the assessment context, emanating from the CRC, Elwood and Lundy argued that "those with responsibility for assessment will need to ensure that: the best interests of the child are a primary consideration in decision-making; that children are offered opportunities to participate meaningfully through the decision-making process; and that opportunities to learn, progress and succeed will be offered to children equally."[6] Figure I.1 shows three interrelated questions that those concerned with the assessment of children should consistently address.[7]

While these questions may be particularly salient in the context of assessments that result in high-stakes decisions (e.g., accountability, certification, or placement), they are not the only situations in which the three questions have significance. The perspective taken in this book is that, for a number of reasons, all three are as important, if not even more so, in the everyday work of teachers. First, teachers need to ensure that all children are served equally well by their assessment practices. In the classroom setting, this does not necessarily mean that all children receive identical or standardized assessment practices. Quite the contrary. The CRC's emphasis on equal and meaningful participation in learning requires that teachers systematically make provisions and maximize opportunities for individual students to display the nature and quality of their thinking so teachers can make proximate decisions about how to secure progress in the best interests of each child. Without due attention to the learning needs of each student, the primary consideration of children's best interests will likely not be fully

FIGURE I.1
Children's Rights Assessment Framework

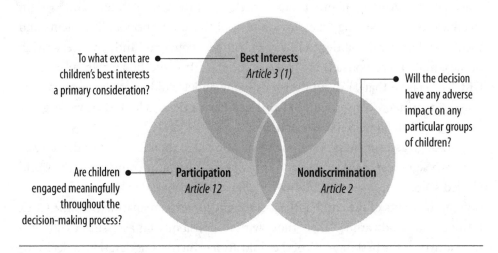

addressed. In this vein, chapters in the book will explore the central importance of immediate and systematic information about how each student's learning is developing. Teachers will not be able to ensure that all students have the chance to move forward without this information.

Second, if the question about student engagement throughout the decision-making process is to be taken seriously, students cannot just be given results of assessments and told what the decisions based on them will be, for example, class groupings, specific homework, targeted intervention, extra work, summer school, redoing tasks, or listening to the lesson again. When combined with the ideas of personalized learning and serving students' best interests, addressing the question about student engagement in decisions leads to practices that situate students as equal stakeholders in assessment with their teachers. As equal stakeholders, students are not test-result recipients; instead, they are invited to be actively involved in assessment in a variety of ways, all focused on supporting them as learners. This is another perspective that will be elaborated in the following chapters.

Finally, if teachers do not make a point of consistently inquiring into the nature and status of their students' learning, and subsequently take action based on the information that is intended to move each student's learning forward, then there is a real possibility that some students or even subgroups of students will be adversely impacted. This view will recur throughout the book.

At the conclusion of their discussion on the child's rights in assessment, Elwood and Lundy proposed that assessment should be considered as "an enabling factor in delivering the aims of education for all children, irrespective of context or circumstances."[8] Their proposition is fully embraced in this book, the main thesis of which is that formative assessment, conceived of as a process of inquiry and action, is a primary "enabling factor" in students' learning.

A significant outcome of formative assessment as an enabling factor in students' learning is personalized learning. The following section presents a discussion of what personalized learning entails.

PERSONALIZED LEARNING

The view of learning advanced from a "personalized" perspective is that learning is an active, social process designed to build student independence through interaction, intervention, stimulation, and collaboration.[9] The development of students' independence in learning implies a growing capacity for self-regulation: a process of taking control of and evaluating one's own knowledge, learning behavior, and strategies.[10] Self-regulation can usefully be conceived of as involving several layers. In Boekaerts' influential model, there is an inner core concerned with the regulation of cognitive processing and the selection of cognitive strategies, a second layer of metacognitive knowledge and skills used in the direction of learning, and an outer layer concerned with the choice of goals and the allocation of time and effort in their pursuit.[11] Although self-regulation is frequently contrasted with external regulation stemming from the structure of classroom tasks and instructional interventions, it is appropriated from, and emerges within, the context of a complicated classroom context comprising educational tasks, teacher interventions, peer interactions, and assessment activities. For this reason, the process of learning in classrooms can fundamentally be considered "as a process of co-regulation or of shared regulation."[12] In this process of shared regulation, students are involved with their teacher and each other in goal setting, monitoring learning, and developing autonomy.

Although teachers and peers can assist learning, in the end, no one other than the student can actually do the learning. Personalized learning concerns the development of learning dispositions, habits, attitudes, and identities that enable students to become lifelong learners, a prerequisite for success in an ever-changing world. Formative assessment practices can significantly contribute to the development of personalized learning. The theme of personalized learning will recur throughout the book.

As the book title makes clear, formative assessment involves both inquiry and action. Both teachers and students, sharing joint responsibility for learning, engage in inquiry and action in distinct, yet complementary, ways. In the next section, we examine elements of the practice of formative assessment and the shared responsibilities of teachers and students in more detail.

ELEMENTS OF FORMATIVE ASSESSMENT PRACTICE

Erickson refers to formative assessment as a continual "taking stock" of learning by "paying first-hand observational attention to students during the ongoing course of instruction."[13] The purpose of this "continual taking stock of learning" is to "form new learning."[14] Forming new learning requires teachers to intentionally generate evidence about learning, and to interpret the evidence in order make decisions about pedagogical action to close the "gap" between the learners current status and desired goals.[15] Such action can include making adaptations to instruction and providing feedback to students that gives them hints or cues so they can take steps on their own to progress in learning. This element of formative assessment practice is central to the work of teaching.

A second element of formative assessment is pivotal in the work of learning. When students understand the goal being aimed for and are assisted to develop the skills to make judgments about their progress in relation to that goal, they come to establish a repertoire of operational strategies to regulate their own learning. If students lack the resources to monitor their own learning and take corrective action, then they remain overwhelmingly dependent on teacher feedback as the primary resource for learning. As a consequence, they will inevitably be hindered in their capacity to develop as self-sustaining lifelong learners. In formative assessment, students' clarity about learning goals and success criteria as indicators of progress are essential to the ongoing monitoring of their own learning and the development of self-regulation skills. In this way, the students themselves are also engaged in continual *taking stock* of learning as well as in *forming* new learning.

In sum, the core constituents of formative assessment are:

- Clear learning goals and success criteria
- Evidence gathering and interpretation
- Responsive pedagogical action
- Student involvement

Let us now turn to a classroom vignette to consider how, when these fundamental elements of formative assessment are enacted, teachers can be responsive to individual students and personalized learning can be enabled.

Ms. Lee teaches in a school in downtown Los Angeles, close to Skid Row. In her class, she has thirty first- and second-grade students who are all recipients of free or reduced lunches, and over ninety percent of them are designated English learners. In this lesson, the students are learning about representing and solving problems involving addition and subtraction. Ms. Lee begins by connecting the focus of the lesson to what the students have previously learned. She discusses the specific learning goal for the lesson, as well as the criteria that she and the children will use to decide if they are meeting the goal. This is what she has written on the white board:

> Today, we are learning how to represent our understanding of a one-step word problem and to use a strategy to solve the problem.
>
> The criteria that will guide your learning are:
>
> - I can identify what the word problem is asking me to do.
> - I can use a math strategy to help me solve the problem (I can use appropriate math tools to help me, if I need them).
> - I can give an explanation of my thinking using accurate math vocabulary.

Then she introduces what she terms an "active engagement strategy" where students are involved in peer conversations about a given story problem. This is the problem they discuss.

> Jorge collected 730 stamps. After giving some stamps to his friends, he had 645 stamps left. How many stamps did he give to his friends?

Guided by Ms. Lee, the children discuss the problem and identify the action and problem (in her terms, "the who?" and "the what?").

The children cease their conversations and Ms. Lee begins a mini-lesson, by discussing with the students what the problem requires them to do, and then she invites them to consider how the problem can be solved. After a period of quiet thinking time, she asks specific children to share with the whole class different ways in which the problem can be solved and reminds them about the success criteria they previously discussed. As individual students share their problem-solving ideas, their peers have opportunities to provide feedback to them about their method and their reasoning. Ms. Lee uses these exchanges during the mini-lesson to gauge the level of student understanding about representing and solving the problem. Following this, Ms. Lee asks the students to "turn and talk" in twos or threes to discuss other ways they might be able to represent and solve the problem.

While they are engaged in discussion, she visits each group in turn to listen in and to ask clarifying questions, such as "What is the action in the problem?" and "Did the second number increase or decrease? Why?" This is yet another opportunity for her to assess student understanding. Based on what she has heard in the student discussions, she decides she needs to clarify which quantity in the problem is the unknown. She then returns to the lesson goal and success criteria and once again reviews them with the children to make sure they are clear about their intended learning.

After the mini-lesson, students work independently on representing and solving problems. Here is the problem they are asked to solve.

> Rico had a bag of marbles. He gave _____ marbles to his younger brother Cruz. Now he has _____ marbles left. How many marbles did Rico have to start with?
>
> (5, 13)   (43, 52)   (227, 332)

The numbers in parentheses represent differing levels of knowledge about place value. Different students work on different numbers in the problem, depending on their current level of understanding of place value as determined by Ms. Lee. Students are also involved in selecting the numbers they will work on by deciding on a "just right" number. Ms. Lee and the children have developed a set of criteria that they use to choose numbers that are at the right level for them—not too easy and not too challenging. Of course, Ms. Lee monitors very closely the choice of numbers, but finds that the students have effectively determined what is right for each of them.

While the children work independently, Ms. Lee engages in one-on-one conferences with a number of students. These student conferences have been predetermined based on previous discussions, observations of student activity, and review of work products. During the conference, she reviews their work products and asks strategic questions designed to probe their thinking and encourage them to consider how they solved problems and also to justify their approach, for example, she asks "Why did you select that strategy to solve the problem?" or "Do you think this is the most efficient way to solve the problem? Why?"

Ms. Lee responds to each of the students based on the evidence she has elicited from the students' work and her interaction with them. Her responses include clarifying a student's explanation, a targeted teaching point to either clear up a misunderstanding or move a student to a higher level of understanding, and specific feedback to a student to provide a hint or cue that the student can use to progress. She writes the feedback on a sticky note so the student has it for reference when returning to independent work. For example, for one student she writes, "Can you think of a number sentence that would match your visual representation?" and for another she writes, "I'd like you to think of another strategy and compare it with this strategy to decide which one is more efficient and why." At the end of the conference, she asks the students to evaluate themselves in relation to the success criteria and discusses with them their self-assessment. In these conversations, she asks the students to explain why they think they have met the goal, or why they haven't and what help they think they need. She values the students' own judgments and finds them a useful source of insight into how they think about their own learning. In each of the conferences, she makes notes about what was discussed, what her response was, and where she thinks the student needs to go next in learning.

Toward the end of their work time, the children complete a self-reflection about their learning that day. In this reflection, they record any challenges, successes, and what they think they need to do next. The lesson ends with a plenary session where Ms. Lee chooses an example of two strategies she has observed, which she turns into a teachable moment for all students.

At the end of the day, Ms. Lee considers the information she has gained from several sources of data during the lesson: the students' work products (their representations and problem-solving strategies), the feedback students provided to each other during the mini-lesson, her interactions with each small group during the mini-lesson, her conference notes, her observations, and students' own reflections on their learning. She uses the evidence she has from the students to make decisions about what levels students have reached, where she needs to begin her math instruction the following day, and which students she will meet with one-on-one. She also reflects on the targeted instruction she provided during the lesson to decide if she needs to revisit some of these teaching points with the whole class, with small groups or with specific individuals.

Ms. Lee's first step in accommodating the diversity of learners in her class is the attention she pays to the learning goal and the tasks students are asked to undertake. She wants all students to have the opportunity to engage in solving problems, but recognizes that, while all her students have an understanding of addition, there is a range of understanding in relation to place value among her class. She accommodates this range by differentiating the numbers that students will work on. She knows which are the appropriate numbers for each student because of the information she has obtained in prior lessons.

As the lesson vignette develops, we can see Ms. Lee consistently engaged in a process of inquiry through which she continuously "takes stock" of learning as it unfolds. Ms. Lee has not left her moments of inquiry to chance but rather has carefully structured a range of opportunities within the lesson to generate the evidence she needs. With the information she gains, she is able to make a range of pedagogical responses, scaffolding learning and providing feedback intended to advance learning for each student. As a result, the children are not treated as a homogeneous group that progresses in lockstep. She does not teach to the middle of the class and hope everyone will get something out of the lesson; nor does she focus on the learning needs of a subset of students with the idea that exposure to the targeted instruction designed to meet these students' specific needs will somehow benefit the rest of the students in the class. Even though Ms. Lee's students spend time during the lesson working in groups, her focus is always on making sure the best interests of each child are being served and that progress for each child is secured. In short, she makes sure that learning is individually sized. Important to note here is that in Ms. Lee's class, individually sized learning does not mean that she provides one-on-one instruction for each of her thirty students. Instead, she uses all the resources available to her in different group and task structures to respond to the needs of individuals.

Important to notice, too, is the role the students play in the lesson. Far from being passive recipients of what Ms. Lee has to teach, they play an active role in their own and each other's learning. To help them do this, Ms. Lee first provides the students with clear expectations about what the day's math learning entails in the form of the learning goal and success criteria. With these expectations in mind, they are then involved in decision-making about their learning level with the use of the "just right number" criteria. As the lesson develops, the students use the learning goal and success criteria to reflect on their own learning, to evaluate how their learning progresses, and to think about where they need to go next. Students also support each other's learning through the provision of feedback during the mini-lesson. Ms. Lee has taught them how to provide feedback that is constructive and helps their classmates learn in whole-group and small-group settings. Lest some of them should need reminders about how to do this, Ms. Lee has given them a range of conversation prompts that they keep inside their math folders, which are categorized into "asking for clarification," "disagreeing," and "expressing an opinion." Through their self-evaluation and peer feedback, students begin to reflect on their own learning, an essential element of personalized learning.

With this classroom vignette in mind, let us now return to the questions relating to the rights of the child in assessment. In Ms. Lee's assessment, the best interests of the child are a primary consideration. She strives to ensure that she has the information she needs to keep each student's learning on track, and to assist each one in the successful accomplishment of the intended learning. Her students are given the opportunity to engage meaningfully in the decision-making process: they decide on the numbers that present the just right level of challenge in problem solving and they evaluate their own learning, determining successes and challenges and what they need to do next. Note that Ms. Lee has not abrogated her responsibilities as their teacher, but rather treats the students as partners in guiding learning, a necessity if the phrase "meaningfully engaged" is to have any potency. Above all, children are offered opportunities to learn, progress, and succeed equally. No individual student or subgroup is privileged above others. It is sometimes believed that formative assessment is mainly applicable for struggling students. This is not the case. Formative assessment is for all students so that teachers can build on what students already know to move them incrementally through from their current state of learning to a more advanced state.

In accord with the children's rights perspective on assessment, being given the opportunity to learn, progress, and succeed equally is dependent on skilled teachers who are able to individualize learning, not standardize it. As we noted earlier, one-size learning definitely does not fit all, and formative assessment is the route to learning that is individually sized. As Jim Pellegrino and Robert Glaser observed "what matters most in formative assessment is the careful probing and analysis of student understandings, which leads to sensitive student-specific adjustments in the overall learning environment, thereby influencing individual learning trajectories."[16]

There is clear research evidence that when the principles of formative assessment exemplified in this vignette are effectively implemented, they lead to improvements in students' attainment.[17] As Black, Wilson, and Yao pointed out, this is hardly surprising given that the principles of learning that underlie formative assessment practice are well established and supported by cognitive theory and research.[18] In the next section, we examine more closely these principles of learning, which will be anchor points for the discussion of formative assessment throughout this book.

PRINCIPLES OF LEARNING AND FORMATIVE ASSESSMENT

Working on the Edge of Learning

As we have discussed, formative assessment is concerned not solely with the actual level of performance, the levels of attainment that students have reached, but with anticipating future possibilities.[19] This stance derives from Vygotsky's view that instruction "must be aimed not so much at the ripe as at the ripening functions."[20] To aim instruction at the "ripening functions" teachers need information about a student's *zone of nearest development* (also termed *the zone of proximal development* or *ZPD*), described by Vygotsky as "those processes in the development of the same functions, which, as they are not mature today, still are already on their way, are already growing through, and already tomorrow will bear fruit."[21]

Vygotsky considered that maturing cognitive structures are unlikely to fully mature without interaction with others, emphasizing the social processes of learning in which learners collaborate with more knowledgeable others.[22] In this regard, he distinguished between two levels of development: 1) the level of actual development that the learner has already reached, the level at which the learner is capable of solving problems independently; and 2) the level of potential development (the ZPD), the level that the learner is capable of reaching under the guidance of a more knowledgeable other. He further proposed that learning occurs on two planes: first on the social level, between people (interpsychological), and second, on the individual level, within the learner (intrapsychological).

Learning on the interpsychological plane occurs through a process of *scaffolding* when the more knowledgeable other (a teacher or a peer) provides support through a process of interaction.[23] This assistance helps the learner work in and through the ZPD, and as the learner's competence grows, the scaffolding is gradually reduced until the learner can function independently.[24]

Viewed within Vygotsky's framework, the process of formative assessment requires that teachers work at the "edge" of learning. They generate and interpret data about the ZPD, the bandwidth of competence that currently exists and which learners can navigate with assistance to move to a more advanced state of understanding or skill.[25] This is what contingent learning entails and is exactly what Ms. Lee is endeavoring to do with her students. Through a process of data gathering, she is able to gain information about each student's current learning status so that she can provide the necessary assistance to increase her students' independent competence. The successful accomplishment of this "edge work" constitutes a core characteristic of formative assessment practice.[26]

In addition, it is important to note that in Ms. Lee's classroom, she is not the only agent active in the development of learning. Students are resources for each other as well. By carefully structuring contexts in which students can provide feedback to their peers (e.g., the conversation prompts and the feedback opportunities during the discussion time), Ms. Lee enables her students to take full advantage of other partners in learning and, in the process, share available cognitive resources within the classroom community.[27]

Metacognition

Cognitive theory notes the central role of metacognition in learning.[28] Metacognition has been variously described as "the ability to monitor one's current level of understanding and decide when it is not adequate"; the "human capacity to be self-reflective, to consider *how* one thinks and knows; it directs attention to what has been assimilated and understood, and the ways in which this relates to the process of learning"; and "cognition that reflects on, monitors, or regulates first-order cognition."[29] In a further elaboration, Bereiter and Scardamalia noted that metacognition also includes self-regulation, the ability to orchestrate one's learning by planning and correcting errors when appropriate.[30] Self-regulation is a necessary aspect of effective intentional learning. These descriptions all share the idea that metacognition is an active process, which enables learners to make judgments and take regulative steps with respect to their own learning. Through metacognitive processes, then, students become conscious of their learning and thus are able to develop control over how they learn.[31] Kuhn suggested that metacognition emerges early in life, and follows an extended developmental course during which it increasingly operates under the individual's conscious control.[32]

When effectively implemented, formative assessment practices can assist in the development of metacognition and support students to take control of their own learning. Returning to the vignette of Ms. Lee's classroom, we see several instances in which students are actively involved in developing metacognitive processes. First, they are clear about the learning goal and the criteria they can use to actively monitor their success in achieving the goal. Clarity about the purpose of learning and the indicators for monitoring its emergence are essential for metacognition.[33] Second, students take responsibility for deciding which numbers were the best "fit" for them to work with, which involves judging their current level of learning and what a next step might be. Third, Ms. Lee models the metacognitive process by asking students to consider how they solved problems and why they approached the problem in the way they did.[34] Fourth, at the end of each of her conferences, Ms. Lee asks the students to evaluate their own learning in relation to the success criteria. Finally, at the conclusion of the lesson, all students conduct a reflection on how they thought they had fared in learning, noting successes, challenges, and any assistance they needed in order to progress.

Although still in the earliest of primary grades, Ms. Lee's students are clearly beginning the process of personalizing learning. Ms. Lee's classroom is saturated with opportunities through which the children can begin the process of taking control over how they learn, and simultaneously use their metacognitive knowledge and skills to navigate the learning process.

Ms. Lee's classroom embodies many formative assessment practices that research synthesized by Black and Wiliam has shown can propel student learning.[35] In this book, these practices are described and exemplified for a range of audiences.

WHO SHOULD READ THIS BOOK?

This book is intended for those who are interested in supporting student learning by making formative assessment an integral part of classroom practice. Teachers, regardless of their stage of implementing formative assessment, will find the book a resource for developing and refining their practices. Administrators can use the book to expand their knowledge about the practice of formative assessment and consider how to assist teachers and their students to become skilled in formative assessment. This book can be a source that sheds light on the theory and practice of formative assessment, with specific examples of how it operates in classrooms as well as models and points of reflection for those responsible for the initial preparation of teachers. Finally, the book can help policy makers develop a clear picture of the interrelationship of teaching, learning, and assessment, and the policies that can enable the practice of formative assessment to benefit all students irrespective of context or circumstances.

OVERVIEW OF THE CHAPTERS

The chapters are framed in terms of the preceding discussion on children's rights and personalized learning. Each one focuses on a particular aspect of formative assessment, provides practical examples of formative assessment in action, and considers the knowledge and skills teachers need for successful implementation. A brief description of each chapter's content follows.

> **Chapter 1:** Drawing from a sociocultural perspective, the chapter examines the classroom as a community of practice in which learning and formative assessment take place. The chapter considers how teachers and students contribute to this community of practice in terms of roles they assume, their respective

goals and practices, and norms for interaction they adopt. The chapter also introduces the idea of signature pedagogies for formative assessment.

These range from developing shared expectations about what assessment entails, to the established routines needed for successful formative assessment, to the active engagement of students in the construction of their identity as learners.

Chapter 2: This chapter begins with a discussion of some of the reasons for the current interest in the idea of learning progressions, followed by a variety of definitions of learning progressions and an analysis of the dominant themes that emerge from the literature. The chapter includes descriptions of research-based and empirically validated progressions as the basis for assessment. While recognizing that such progressions are desirable, the chapter offers some practical suggestions for how teachers can create their own progressions to support formative assessment.

Chapter 3: This chapter connects to the "inquiry" aspect of formative assessment. It focuses on the purpose of gathering proximate evidence about learning with extensive examples of evidence collection strategies.

Chapter 4: Connecting to the "action" aspect of formative assessment, this chapter extends the discussion from the previous chapter about the purpose of gathering evidence with a specific focus on the responsive actions that teachers will take—scaffolding and feedback to students—to advance learners from where they are to reach desired goals.

Chapter 5: This chapter continues the "inquiry and action" theme of the book, with specific reference to the student perspective. It begins by referencing the ideas expressed in the introduction in relation to a students' rights approach to assessment. The chapter emphasizes the need for students to learn for themselves, not only to be successful in school, but also to be prepared for a potential lifetime of learning.

Chapter 6 (coauthored with E. Caroline Wylie): The concluding chapter presents the view that effective implementation of formative assessment cannot occur without policy support for the practice. Drawing on lessons learned from a variety of countries (including Australia, Canada, England, Finland, France, New Zealand, Norway and Scotland), the chapter considers policies that could create the conditions for widespread implementation of formative asssssment practices.

CHAPTER 1

Forming Communities of Practice

Successful formative assessment takes place in the context of classrooms where students and teachers are participants in a community of practice.[1] While the term "community of practice" is a relatively new one, the phenomenon it refers to is age-old; it signals the formation of groups organized around the use of a common set of practices, procedures, and standards deployed in pursuit of some goal.[2] For example, a group of artisans form a community of practice and communicate those practices, procedures, and standards to apprentices seeking to become an artisan. A group of musicians who play together on an informal basis also form a community, and by the way the musicians operate together, they convey their procedures and practices to newcomers to the group. New group members in both the artisans' and the musicians' groups are apprenticed into the group in the sense that they will not immediately have a clear grasp of the groups' ways of operating. However, over time, new members will come to adopt the groups' practices, procedures, and standards as they consolidate their group membership.

Inherent in the idea of a community of practice is that when individuals participate in the community, the collective practices of the community are the product of actions by its members, and thus mutually codetermined by the participant individuals.[3] So, for example, the practices of one group of apprentice weavers may be different from another. While they all acquire the same knowledge and skill set, how they operate together in their respective groups is determined by each group as a whole. Similarly, when a new musician joins an already formed group, he will gradually adopt the practices of the group, but by virtue of his membership will also influence those same practices.

When group members mutually codetermine their collective practices, they do more than form a common approach to knowledge building. In an insightful observation, Etienne Wenger noted that participating in anything from a playground clique or a work team is both a kind of action and a form of belonging that shape not only what the participants do, but also who they are and how they interpret what they do.[4] Participating in a classroom community is no different. Students do not only acquire subject matter knowledge, they also acquire the ability to act as a learner among other learners. As Jerome Bruner once observed, students do not just simply learn *about*, they also learn to *be*.[5] And as Bruner's comment implies, acting as a learner within a community of practice shapes the student's identity as a learner and this identity, in turn, is reflected in the perceptions and behaviors of other class members.[6] It is for this reason that Greeno and colleagues suggested that learning environments and activities need to be organized so that students can acquire basic skills, knowledge, and conceptual understanding not in isolation but rather in ways that contribute both to the students' development of positive identities as learners and as more effective participants in the social practices of their learning communities in schools.[7]

In this chapter we explore the idea of communities of practice for formative assessment. In such communities, teachers and students gather and act upon information about each student's learning status so as to advance all participants' learning on a continuous basis, and they support each other in the development of students' identities as committed learners. We begin by considering the notion of "situated" formative assessment. There follows a discussion of signature pedagogies, ways in which teachers enable students to become participants a community of practice. The chapter ends with a discussion of the knowledge and skills teachers need to engage in signature pedagogies for formative assessment.

SITUATED FORMATIVE ASSESSMENT

In his 1902 book, *The Child and the Curriculum,* John Dewey, a philosopher and psychologist, and arguably one of the foremost educational thinkers of all time, proposed that learning should not be thought of as an individualized process of knowledge acquisition because "all activity takes place in a medium, a situation, and with reference to its conditions."[8] In anticipation of the concept of a community of practice, Dewey also stressed that "collateral learning," learning about the contextual aspects of an activity, may be more important than the acquisition of the lesson content itself.[9] In the situative approach to learning, which has much in common with Dewey's perspective, the focus is shifted from the behavior and cognition of individuals (e.g., as in the cognitive and behavioral perspectives) to a focus on cognitive agents interacting with each other. Instead of constructing understanding or developing skills by oneself, the situative approach treats knowledge as distributed among individuals and their environment, including the objects, artifacts, tools, and communities that comprise the learning context.[10]

In a further development of Dewey's line of thinking, the situative approach also proposes that learning is a process of "enculturation" in which learners are provided with opportunities to observe and develop competencies within a community of practice.[11] Learning in communities of practice enables participants to develop contextualized competencies that incorporate the learning tools, practices, and social-interactional capacities that are valued within the specific community. For example, when children observe others reading and writing and understand the purposes and value of reading and writing, they want to become members of the literate community so they are able to participate and interact with the world of text. To do so, they learn the tools of the community (manipulating symbols to communicate meaning), the practices of the community (conveying and acquiring messages through written text), and the social interactional capacities (ways of discussing text with others to access meaning or convey appreciation). As Dewey advocated, participation in this literate community becomes both a process and a goal of learning.

In classroom practice, ideas from the situative perspective have led to two main outcomes: participant-oriented learning practices and "cognitive apprenticeship" approaches. Participant-oriented practices include classroom discussions not only to promote students' learning of content but also to encourage their learning of how to participate in the discourse practices that organize the discussions. For example, students learn how to solve problems through learning to participate in the discourse of math problem solving. Similarly, they learn the practices of scientific investigation by learning to participate in the associated science discourse of investigation. In the "cognitive apprenticeship" approach, teachers do not solely engage in didactic teaching but rather in observation and coaching while students carry out a variety of tasks and activities.[12] For instance, in the case of math problem solving, while students are engaged in the task, teachers observe, ask questions, and make suggestions to support learning.

A situative perspective regards all teaching and learning as socially, temporally, and locationally contextualized: it mandates that the design of the learning environment is one in which students can participate in the practices of inquiry and learning, and are supported in developing personal identities as confident, committed, and capable learners.[13] It follows, then, that assessment integrated into the process of teaching and learning will also be situated. Situated formative assessment will arise from the individual actions of participants in the classroom community and their joint shaping of routinized behaviors, interactional patterns, and activities. These social practices operate as the DNA of the community, the coded instructions that allow formative assessment to be a shared endeavor. It is the teacher who must take primary responsibility for making sure that these practices are encoded into the daily life of the classroom. In the next section, we will discuss how this encoding is achieved through the adoption of signature pedagogies for formative assessment.

SIGNATURE PEDAGOGIES

In the context of professional learning, Shulman introduced the idea of "signature pedagogies."[14] These are types of teaching that organize the fundamental ways in which future practitioners, for example, medical students, law students, and education students, are taught for their new professions. In these signature pedagogies, novices in the profession are "instructed in three fundamental dimensions to professional work—*to think, to perform, to act with integrity*" (Shulman's italics).[15] For instance, one of the signature pedagogies for law students is that they are taught to review previous legal cases so as to understand precedent. Similarly, one of the signature pedagogies for medical students is that from the start of their training they are taught to review patients' cases during hospital rounds. Another is that they are instructed in the specific organization of rounds so that they do not waste time organizing themselves every time they enter a patient's room.

Shulman did not conceive of signature pedagogies in relation to the pedagogy that classroom teachers employ with their students. However, the idea of signature pedagogies is applicable to the pedagogies that teachers engage in to create and sustain communities of practice for formative assessment. To help us consider teachers' signature pedagogies for formative assessment, let us first consider several vignettes of classroom practice.

Vignette 1

A high school science teacher begins her series of lessons on understanding the motor effect with an activity in which students work in groups to match cards that feature ideas related to magnetic fields and currents.[16] To complete the activity, students are to use their prior knowledge and make connections between ideas they will later draw on in exploring the motor effect further.

In addition to getting information about the knowledge that students can most easily recall, the teacher is interested in how and if differences of opinion among the students can be resolved. During the activity, students discuss their opinions and challenge each other's ideas while the teacher circulates, listening to the discussion.

Next, based on their work with the cards, students are asked to make a small motor out of simple components provided by the teacher to involve students in thinking about fundamental concepts. Here, the teacher's primary interest is in how the students express their thinking to each other as it develops, identifying as they do so the interaction between magnetic fields and currents. While the students work together, the teacher engages with groups, asking them to explain their thinking and intervening to build on the ideas that emerge. Students are also asked to draw a diagram of their motor with explanatory notes. This will be a resource for the teacher and students to use to discuss present levels of understanding and to plan the next steps.

Vignette 2

In a middle school social studies class, the students are beginning a study of the fundamental economic concepts of supply and demand, as well as the role incentives and profit play in a competitive market system.[17] During the previous day's lesson, the students discussed the concept of incentives in economic and noneconomic contexts. In today's lesson, the teacher wants to see how well they understand the idea of incentives, and asks them to work independently to write two paragraphs applying the concept of incentives to both economic and noneconomic decisions in their own life. Before the students begin the task, the teacher asks the students to write either an "I," "C," or "A" in their notebooks. This notation system is one the students use regularly. A means "I am not ready to start my work, I need more assistance"; C means "I have a clarifying question I need to ask before I can begin"; and I means "I am ready to go and work independently."

The majority of the students write the letter I. The teacher asks these students to start their writing and the others to gather together in a carpeted area of the classroom. Starting with those who need to ask clarifying questions, the teacher quickly answers two students' questions and four students leave the area to begin their assignment. Then the teacher asks the remaining students what they still need assistance with. One student says she is not sure how to link the idea of incentives to her own life and the others agree that they are also having difficulty with this idea. There then follows a discussion in which the teacher goes over the idea of incentives and asks a number of questions to prompt the students' thinking, for example, "Whose incentive is stronger—a worker who is paid for the number of pieces he or she produces each day or a worker who is given a share in the company's profits?" The students respond and the teacher asks them to give reasons for their responses.

At this point in the discussion, several students get up and leave the area to begin their work. They have made the decision that they are ready to work independently now. The few remaining students engage in a discussion with the teacher about how these ideas could relate to their own experiences and after a few minutes all the students say they now understand and can complete the assignment. As they leave, the teacher quickly makes notes about who needed assistance and what was discussed.

Vignette 3

During an upper-elementary lesson on examining reasons and evidence an author can use to support particular points in a text, students read two passages from different authors and are asked to write on a sticky note an explanation of how the authors have used evidence to support a specific point.[18] Once the students have written their ideas, they stick the note on the white board at the front of the class. The teacher then carefully orchestrates a discussion of the responses (without revealing who wrote each one), asking students questions to help them evaluate each explanation, for example "In what way does this response explain how the evidence is related to the author's claim?" As the discussion progresses, it becomes evident to everyone that the class as a whole is still not clear about what constitutes supporting evidence and they all agree that they will need to spend more time on reading persuasive texts and discussing how authors use evidence.

Although the three vignettes differ in terms of the grade levels and the subject matter reflected, taken as a whole, four signature pedagogies emerge. These are:

1. Establishing routinized and mutually understood practices of behavior and interaction;
2. Enabling student agency;

3. Revealing students' current learning status; and

4. Modeling values and attitudes.

Next, we examine each one more closely.

Establishing Routinized and Mutually Understood Practices

The first signature pedagogy involves creating routines and behaviors that enable both students and teachers to participate in a community of practice for formative assessment.

In the high school classroom example, students collaborated in a series of tasks: they used cards to build representations of the electromagnetic processes involved, discussed those representations and evaluated and critiqued each other's ideas, and finally collaborated in constructing an electric motor. Through all of these activities, the joint development of students' thinking was part of a process in which individual understandings were expanded and enriched. In addition, the teacher played a role in the development of students' thinking by listening carefully to their emerging ideas and intervening in ways that built on the ideas.

In the middle school social studies vignette, the use of letter categories is a practice that is routinely incorporated into the students' learning environment as one way to monitor their own understanding and decide when they need assistance. The responsibility for making the decision does not rest with the teacher, but rather with the students, as does the responsibility for determining when they have sufficient understanding to complete their task. The teacher engages the students who need assistance in a discussion through which students collectively increase individual understanding. It is worth noting in this example that students are nonjudgmental about their own learning status and that of others. Students recognize that levels of understanding will vary during the course of the lesson and that in their classroom community it is an individual's responsibility to decide if more assistance is needed and that there is a group responsibility to support peers in their learning.

In the third vignette, the elementary English language arts (ELA) example, the students engage in a collective, public evaluation of their learning, through which they are able to determine what the class as a whole needs to do next. Again, the authority for making the evaluation does not rest solely with the teacher. Instead, all the students take responsibility for making decisions because they are provided with the tools and practices to contribute to a shared understanding of their learning and what they need to do to progress.

The regularity and recurrence of the kind of participant structures these teachers have put in place enable the students to become socialized, through joint activity, into the practices of formative assessment. They have taken on participatory identities in the classroom that correspond to the ways in which they are expected and entitled to participate in the interaction.[19]

Enabling Student Agency

Students' agency is central to personalized learning, which, as discussed in the introduction, involves the development of self-regulation and autonomy as learners. In addition, student agency relates to the children's rights perspective on assessment in that their views are given due weight in all matters affecting them. In the context of formative assessment, students' agency refers to their making judgments about their own learning and deciding on their own, or in collaboration with the teacher and peers, the action they need to take to move learning forward. This topic is elaborated on in chapter 5. The development of students' agency is a counterpart to the growth of their identities as confident and capable learners.

Exercising agency in formative assessment means that students do not simply rely on teachers' pronouncements about their learning status and what they need to do next, but are active in forming their own judgments. Teacher pedagogy to enable students' agency in learning is closely intertwined with the pedagogy of creating mutually understood routines, practices, and behaviors discussed previously. Student involvement in the assessment process through the established participant structures of the classroom provides the opportunities for agency but does not constitute agency itself. Students must be supported and guided within these opportunities to make determinations about where they and their peers are in their learning and how they can make progress. These processes are essential for students to learn how to learn.

In the vignettes we see many kinds of student agency in the assessment process. In the high school vignette, the teacher and students discuss the diagrams and associated explanations and make joint decisions about what should happen next; in the middle-school social-studies vignette, the students are responsible for determining their own level of understanding; and in the elementary (ELA) vignette, students and the teacher collaborate to evaluate the class' learning. In each case, the teachers create the requisite participant structures for student involvement, and they also give the students authority to make judgments about their own and other's learning. In so doing, the teachers do not abdicate their expertise in interpreting what students say or write to indicate their learning status. Instead, through scaffolding and shared reflection in the context of the authentic practice of formative assessment, they invite students to join them as apprentices in the development of their own expertise.[20]

Revealing Students' Current Learning Status

Let us take a moment to recall two of the key ideas of formative assessment that were presented in the introduction. First, formative assessment involves the continual taking stock of learning as it develops, a systematic gathering of evidence that can be used to move learning forward. Second, the evidence gathered should help teachers anticipate future possibilities in learning so they can provide the "just right" kind of support required by students to mature understanding, skills, and processes that are on the cusp of developing. It follows, then, that one of the signature pedagogies in formative assessment is eliciting responses from students that reveal their current learning status.[21] This particular pedagogy is evident in all three vignettes.

In the high school example, the teacher created opportunities through tasks and interaction to reveal students' learning. The students' thinking was first elicited through the matching card activity, in which they drew on prior knowledge and resolved differences of opinion through discussion. Next, the students constructed a motor and, while so doing, they explained their thinking to each other. Beyond creating the opportunities through tasks and peer-to-peer discussion, the teacher interacted with the students and responded to the evidence generated by building on emerging ideas in the context of the activity.

In the middle school social studies vignette, the teacher had devised a system for students to make decisions about their own learning status. For those students who had decided they still need assistance, the teacher engaged them in a discussion, using a series of questions to prompt their thinking. Through this process, the teacher both elicited evidence of their thinking and responded in order to help them reach a more developed understanding of the concept and how it could apply to their own lives.

In the final elementary (ELA) example, the teacher elicited evidence of learning by asking for an explanation on a sticky note. In addition, in the process of scaffolding the evaluative discussion, he provided another avenue for students to reveal their thinking to him and to each other, enabling students to reach the final conclusion that they needed to do more work on authors' uses of evidence.

Currently, much of the assessment practice we see in school involves students in a private context; students respond on their own to whatever assessment is administered. In contrast, in the vignettes here, the teacher constructed ways to gather evidence through private, local, and public activity.[22] Public and private activity includes activities that involve only the student, activities that involve small groups of peers, or those that involve the whole class. In the middle-school social-studies vignette, students engaged in private activity, designating their own learning status through a letter in their notebooks. In the high school and social studies vignettes, students were involved in local activity, conversations among small groups of students while they completed tasks. In the elementary school vignette, students participated in the public activity of presentations and discussions involving the whole class. With their students, the teachers in the vignettes established communities of practice for formative assessment that made it possible to distribute the episodes of assessment activity among the task, the teacher, and the students.[23]

In each vignette, evidence gathering was planned and had a place "in the 'rhythm' of the instruction, built-in as part of the constant interaction that is essential to ensure that the teacher and the learner are mutually and closely involved to a common purpose."[24] When assessment is an intrinsic part of instruction, teachers convey the important message to their students that evidence is necessary fuel for continued learning. From the students' point of view, this sets up two expectations. First, they must play a significant role in generating the evidence through the variety of opportunities that they will be given. And second is the expectation that something will happen to progress learning as a result of the evidence gathered. When teachers and students have a shared understanding of what gathering evidence entails, a shared expectation that evidence will be used to further learning, and a shared understanding of their respective roles in the process, a common purpose for formative assessment is forged.

Modeling Values and Attitudes

"They watch us all the time. The students that is. They listen to us, sometimes. They learn from all that watching and listening."[25] This observation by Ted Sizer and Nancy Sizer (Sizers' emphases) leads us to conclude that the final signature pedagogy related to formative assessment inheres in the values and attitudes expressed by what teachers say and do in the classroom. Their expressed values and attitudes influence the development of students' identities as learners, the nature of their participation in the community of practice, and, indeed, the extent to which the class as a whole can function as a community of practice. Paramount here is the teachers' expression of the value of the students, and of attitudes of respect and caring for them. The demonstration of respect and caring serves to create the normative framework for the classroom and contributes to a positive ethos in which formative assessment can occur.

Teachers' demonstration of respect and caring for their students are key elements in creating positive relationships in the classroom.[26] Respect and caring for students as individuals, as well as for the assets and resources they bring to the classroom and the ideas they contribute shape how the students view themselves and others, not to mention the identities they develop as learners. Students watch how teachers relate to them as individuals and to their peers, and they listen to what teachers say and how they say it. Teachers can enable participant structures, but the tenor of the participation will be strongly influenced by the participant models the teacher provides.

In addition, the teacher's demonstration of respect and caring is integral to creating a safe classroom ethos, which, in turn, is essential for formative assessment practice. If students are to reveal their current learning status to their teacher and peers, then they need to feel secure that mistakes, incomplete ideas, or confusion will not be treated as occasions for ridicule or sanctions, but rather as sources of new learning for the individual and the class as a whole.[27] How teachers respond to students provides the cues for how students respond to each other.

Finally, teachers demonstrate respect and caring in not just how they talk to students, but how they listen to them as well. In the context of formative assessment, teachers need to demonstrate interpretive listening, attending closely to what the student is saying so as to understand the student's ideas. Carl Rogers captured the essence of this kind of listening with the idea that it requires a person to "lay aside your own views and values in order to enter another's world without prejudice."[28] Teachers must listen for the sense in students' thinking rather than making judgments about students or about the rightness or wrongness of the response.[29] As students are in the process of learning, their ideas may be fragmentary or intermittently grasped, and only by listening for the sense in the idea will the teacher be able to build on it and assist students to reach a more developed understanding.

The teacher's orientation as a listener will convey the value placed on the student's ideas and ultimately on the student as an individual, contributing to the student's identity as a learner in the classroom. It will also provide the model for how students listen to each other during the classroom interactions. Listening without prejudice is a hallmark of a community of practice for formative assessment.

Returning to the vignettes, we can infer the values and attitudes that the three teachers express in the classroom. The fact that students feel safe to share ideas, to discuss opinions, and, particularly, in the middle school social studies vignette to indicate to their peers that they need more assistance is testament to the kind of relationships that have been established, in large part because of the teachers' demonstration of caring and respect. A classroom atmosphere has been created wherein students are able to contribute ideas and reveal their thinking without fear of any negative judgment. The students display the levels of respect and caring to their peers that have been modeled for them by their teachers.

In the vignettes, students carefully listen and respond to each other, a stance shaped by teacher modeling. In the high school vignette, students listened to each other's ideas, challenged them, and resolved differences of opinion. In the middle school vignette, the students listened to each other's responses to the teacher's questions, which serve as a means to develop their individual understanding. In the vignette of the elementary classroom, students also listened to their peers' responses, which led to a common conclusion among the class members.

An interview with a fifth-grade teacher from a school in downtown Los Angeles about her formative assessment practice is instructive in how the values and attitudes of respect and caring are inculcated into the classroom community.

At our school we have a values-based program that teaches students about empathy and respect and the golden rule—behaving toward others as you would like them to behave to you. In the academic setting that becomes very important because there is an expectation of respect and the students are very aware of how they should and should not treat each other. During the lessons a lot of discussion and collaboration takes place. The students feel safe to share, to ask each other questions because that has been modeled to them by me and by also using students as models.[30]

This teacher is explicit about the behaviors she expects from her students and the respect that is emblematic of their relationships. She is also very aware of her role in modeling these behaviors and attitudes for her students to emulate. These expectations and modeling contribute to students' feelings of safety and their willingness to share ideas and ask questions.

Taken together, these four signature pedagogies, establishing routinized and mutually understood practices of behavior and interaction, enabling student agency, revealing students' current learning status, and modeling values and attitudes comprise the ways in which a community of practice for formative assessment is enculturated. The adoption of the pedagogies by teachers stems from their expectations that students can and will learn with and from each other, that students will be actively involved in assessment, and that each student's best interest will be the core work of the community as a whole. In turn, the teachers' expectations are mirrored in the attitudes, behaviors, and expectations shared among the students.

Recall from the introduction that in a children's rights approach to formative assessment, teachers and students are responsible for obtaining and using information in ways that serve the best needs of each student, enabling all of them to progress in learning. Communities of practice in which participants operate with shared expectations and anticipated outcomes, accepted and consistent activities, and social and interactional practices and behaviors provide the context within which information is obtained and used so that each student has the opportunity to succeed. Also, from the standpoint of personalized learning, communities of practice support students in developing learning dispositions, habits, attitudes, and identities that are so important for them in becoming lifelong learners. The signature pedagogies that teachers engage in make possible a community of practice for formative assessment. To be able to enact the signature pedagogies requires teachers to possess certain knowledge and skills. In the final section, we consider the knowledge and skills that will assist teachers to effectively implement the four pedagogies to create a community of practice for formative assessment.

TEACHER KNOWLEDGE AND SKILLS

Teachers in the earlier vignettes did not acquire their abilities to implement the four signature pedagogies overnight. Instead, their skills developed over time as teachers gained specific knowledge, consistently practiced the pedagogies, and reflected about how effectively they implemented the pedagogies. Next, we enumerate the knowledge and skills that teachers should progressively acquire to implement the signature pedagogies.

First, it is important that teachers understand formative assessment as a process of inquiry and action that is embedded in their everyday practice—routine classroom assessment "integrated with pedagogy to maximize its formative potential in promoting learning," which involves the participation of students.[31] For teachers who view assessment as something external, in competition with teaching and learning and that does not require student participation in the process, developing this understanding will involve a considerable shift in their thinking and behavior. The kind of change involved is encapsulated by middle school mathematics teacher, Shawn Morgan, who, when reflecting on his implementation of formative assessment, said "I used to do a lot of *explaining*, but now I do a lot of *questioning*. I used to do a lot of *talking*, but now I do a lot of *listening*. I used to think *about teaching the curriculum*, but now I think *about teaching the student*" (Morgan's emphases).[32] Formative assessment understood in this way serves as the framework for the signature pedagogies we have discussed.

Second, teachers need to create the physical and social environment of the classroom. If students are to engage in collaborative work and have opportunities to work in different configurations to share ideas, exchange opinions, and build their thinking together, then the physical environment must be set up so as to facilitate this range of opportunities, and to enable students to move quickly into different grouping arrangements. We saw this particularly in vignette two, when the students who needed assistance grouped together in a carpeted area of the classroom where the teacher could hold a discussion while the rest of the class worked independently.

Third, creating the social environment requires a fundamental understanding of what constitutes a community of practice for formative assessment. This includes understanding that the teacher and the students have distinct, but complementary, roles in the community; the nature of these roles; and the ways in which they come to be realized in the classroom. Then, teachers need the skills to create opportunities for productive teacher–student and student–student interactions and structure them so that all students have access to the conversations and are able to contribute in substantive ways. Teachers also need the skills to model constructive interactions, which, in combination with the participant opportunities the teacher creates, shape the expectations for student participation in the discourse structures, and for the respectful and caring ethos of the classroom.

Fourth, the pedagogy of revealing students' learning status requires teachers to have the skills to create or devise assessment situations, tasks, observations, and interactions that will provide insights into students' current understanding with respect to the intended learning. These skills include making sure that assessment opportunities are aligned to the learning goal (the construct being addressed), that they are an appropriate representation of the construct and address the important dimensions of the construct, and that they provide tractable information for taking learning further.[33] Teachers must also have the knowledge and skills to place assessment opportunities into the *rhythm of instruction*, at points when both teachers and students will benefit from information to keep learning on track toward the intended goals. The successful deployment of these skills will be dependent on teachers' content knowledge and their pedagogical content knowledge.[34] Without deep knowledge of the concepts and skills students are learning, and optimum ways in which their learning can be revealed, teachers will lack sufficient resources to determine the kinds of opportunities they should create to obtain the required information.

Fifth, teachers need to have the will to find out what students know and well-developed interpretive skills to make sense of the information. For example, they must have the skills of interpretive listening so that they are able to attend carefully to what the students are saying, listening for the sense in students' ideas even when they are not clearly expressed. Careful interpretive listening can lead teachers to understand what students already know and use this current understanding as stepping stones to progress learning. Students who receive the all-too-common diet of recitation questioning (of the Initiation–Response–Evaluation kind), will likely conclude that their teacher is more interested in determining whether their responses are right or wrong than in making sense of their thinking.[35]

Interpretive listening and the use teachers make of what they hear will also depend on the teachers' content knowledge. For example, in addition to the content knowledge related to what students are learning, teachers need to know how students progress through different levels of concept or skills development. In essence, they need to know what the emergence of understanding will sound like or look like in a student response and how an understanding that is in the course of maturing differs from one that is fully consolidated.

Sixth, in a community of practice for formative assessment, students are invited by their teachers to participate in the assessment process and to develop agency with regard to assessment and learning. These invitations require teacher skills in orchestrating discussions with individuals, small groups, or the whole class without foreclosing the students' chances to make judgments about their individual or group learning status and the action they need to take. Related to the "orchestration" skills is teachers' ability to manage the content and pace of lessons so that time is available for reflection and considered discussion. This idea is well captured by one teacher who was asked to respond to changes that had occurred in her classroom practice as she had become more skilled in implementing formative assessment: "I used to do more, but now I do less. Now I work hard to save time for student reflection rather than filling every minute with activity."[36] If teachers are to support student agency in their classrooms, then the maxim "less is more" may serve them well.

Finally, teachers' beliefs about their students and their learning are fundamental to establishing a community of practice in which all students' best interests are taken into account and opportunities to learn, progress, and succeed are offered to children equally.[37] The work of Carol Dweck, in particular, showed the need for teachers to bring to the classroom what they termed a "growth mind-set." By this, Dweck meant the belief that all children can learn and that everyone's intellectual capacity can grow.[38] Dweck contrasted the growth mind-set with a fixed mind-set. Teachers with a fixed mind-set regard learning as dependent on intelligence and view intelligence as fixed and finite. Some students are smart and others are not, and that is just the way things are. Teachers with a growth mind-set see learning as a collaboration with their students, wherein each student will have the chance to grow intellectually. As we have seen in this chapter, learning as collaboration is fundamental to the practice of formative assessment.

Imbuing the classroom with the belief that all students' intellects can be developed leads to feelings among the students of being respected and cared for, which are essential to creating the conditions for formative assessment in a community of practice. Through their behaviors, teachers communicate their growth mind-set to their students so that they can adopt this perspective toward themselves as learners. The formation of a growth mind-set will be instrumental in shaping student identities as confident and capable learners who can function together, in the best interests of all, in the shared endeavor of their community of practice.

In the next chapter, we move from communities of practice to focus on learning progressions and how they can serve as a blueprint for teachers' formative assessment practice.

CHAPTER 2

Applying Learning Progressions

In their landmark review of studies of formative assessment, Black and Wiliam called for "sound models of students' progression in the learning of the subject matter" so that teachers could interpret and respond to assessment evidence in a formative way.[1] Although not specifically focused on formative assessment, their call was echoed by the authors of *Knowing What Students Know* who, in their synthesis of decades of research in cognition, measurement, and psychometrics, proposed that large-scale and classroom assessment should be created from the same underlying model of learning, a progression, as a means to create a comprehensive, coherent, and continuous assessment system.[2] Adding to this perspective, Jim Pellegrino, one of the authors of *Knowing What Students Know,* further argued that "alignment among curriculum, instruction and assessment would be better achieved if all three are derived from a scientifically credible and shared knowledge base about cognition and learning in the subject matter domains."[3]

In recent years, interest in the idea of learning progressions to guide curriculum, instruction, and assessment has grown, particularly, although not exclusively, in the area of science and mathematics.[4] Learning progressions are also called progress variables, progress maps, and learning trajectories.[5] Progressions invite a developmental view of learning because they lay out how expertise develops over a more or less extended period of time, beginning with rudimentary forms of learning and moving through progressively more sophisticated states. When teachers' instruction and formative assessment practices are undergirded by learning progressions, teachers can better use formative assessment to map where individual student's learning currently stands and take steps to move him or her forward.

Students in a class may vary considerably in where their learning is situated on the progression at particular time points. In a striking example, Lee and Ashby showed that the conceptual understandings in history of some 8-year-old students are more advanced than those of many 14-year-olds; other research indicated that instead of learning becoming increasingly homogeneous as students move through school, the spread of achievement increases with age.[6] These findings reinforce the necessity of a children's rights approach to assessment. Students' best interests are served when, in response to assessment information, their learning opportunities are matched to their current learning status and enable them to move forward to a new level. Only when students are able to learn at their current state of readiness can it be said that their best interests are being served, which is a central tenet of a student's rights approach to assessment.

This chapter focuses on learning progressions and how they can serve as a blueprint for teachers' formative assessment practice. We begin by considering learning progressions: what they are and how they are developed. Next, we examine in more detail how progressions can support instruction and formative assessment. This is followed by a discussion of standards and their limitations as supports for formative assessment. Given that there are many gaps in the current suite of researcher-developed learning progressions, the chapter concludes with guidance for how teachers can create progressions to assist them in implementing instruction and formative assessment practice.

WHAT ARE LEARNING PROGRESSIONS?

Consider a learner's acquisition of knowledge of a city. In the early years of life this will be limited to a very local neighborhood, learned through repeated lived experience, and known in a high level of detail, for example, in terms of cracks in the sidewalk, missing bricks in walls, and rusting objects. As the child grows, this neighborhood becomes understood as part of a section of the city. Other sections of the city will be dimly known. A child living in area X might know there is an area of the city called Y, but not where it is located in relation to her, nor any of its specific characteristics. With the passage of time, the child will not only acquire concrete knowledge of other locations, but also the knowledge of how to position them using resources that are not part of her direct lived experience, such as a map. She will learn that freeways connect different areas of the city to one another and will incorporate maps as part of the lived experience of navigation. She will also learn that freeways are arteries for goods and commerce. The child's concept of a city develops from a place where she lives to one in which supplies are sent and goods are shipped. Concurrent with this, the child will also learn the position of the city within a state, and a state within a country, and the country within the world and its geography. Concepts having to do with oceans, continents, atmospheric currents, and tectonic plates will start to be integrated with these understandings, as will a grasp of culture, language, and geopolitics. Within this process, the child's knowledge progresses and ramifies. The child will transition from direct personal experience as a source of information, to the use of maps and charts, to an understanding that satellite navigation can pinpoint any place in the world.

The development of this child's learning embodies the idea of a learning progression: "Kids learn. They start out by being able to do little, and over time they know and can do more, lots more. Their thinking becomes more and more sophisticated" as they respond to instruction and experience in and outside of the school setting.[7]

In elaborations of this succinct formulation, learning progressions have been variously defined as:

- "hypothesized descriptions of the successively more sophisticated ways student thinking about an important domain of knowledge or practice develops as children learn about and investigate that domain over an appropriate span of time";[8]
- "successively more sophisticated ways of thinking about a topic that can be used as templates for the development of curricular and assessment products";[9]
- vertical maps that provide "a description of skills understanding and knowledge in the sequence in which they typically develop: a picture of what it means to 'improve' in an area of learning";[10]
- "a researcher-conjectured, empirically-supported description of the ordered network of constructs a student encounters through instruction (i.e. activities, tasks, tools, forms of interaction and methods of evaluation), in order to move from informal ideas, through successive refinements of representation, articulation, and reflection, towards increasingly complex concepts over time";[11] and

- anchored at one end "by what is known about the concepts and reasoning of children entering school" and by societal expectations at the other end, proposing "*intermediate* understandings between these anchor points that are reasonably coherent networks of ideas and practices and that contribute to building a more mature understanding."[12]

Inherent in each definition of progressions is that learning is envisioned as a process of increasing sophistication in understanding and skills within a domain, beginning with novice levels and moving through increasingly complex stages of competence. For example, a researcher-developed progression for matter and the atomic-molecular theory begins with the idea that objects are made of specific materials and that there are different kinds of materials. It progresses through a number of increasingly sophisticated stages to the idea that the properties of materials are determined by the nature, arrangement, and motion of the molecules of which they are made.[13]

Extant progressions vary in the scope and detail with which they represent the development of expertise. For example, the progression for matter and the atomic-molecular theory is intended to capture developments in students' thinking across grades K–8; whereas, a progression describing the growth of students' understanding of linear measurement spans grades 2 and 3, and a progression designed to show the stages of student thinking about buoyancy (or why things sink and float) is represented at the level of a teaching unit.[14] The emerging body of literature on learning progressions adds dimensions to progressions that are intrinsic to the notion of developing expertise.

First, studies of how expertise develops emphasize the importance of connected knowledge that is organized around the foundational ideas of a discipline.[15] As these studies make clear, conceptual coherence is fundamental to the construction of learning progressions. To this end, progressions generally focus on a "big idea," "core learning," or "essential skill" in a domain and chart the important changes in thinking or skills as interconnected stages of a bigger story. Students initially encounter simpler forms of the idea and are successively carried to new levels of complexity, as a result of experience and instruction, to the ultimate goal of "mastering the connexity" of a body of knowledge.[16] It is important to stress here that, while progressions characterize development, researchers do not view them as developmentally inevitable. Rather, students' development of expertise in a discipline is dependent on effective instruction. The degree to which children are able to engage in particular learning performances and the sequence in which they are able to do so are path dependent: that is, they are strongly shaped by previous opportunities to learn. An additional point worth noting is that while development depends on effective instruction, uneven development may at times constrain progress. For example, a student's level of development in language or reading skills may prevent access to social studies concepts, or a student's lack of the necessary mathematical understanding may inhibit his ability to make sense of science concepts.[17]

Second, in addition to conceptual analysis of the core ideas or major principles required for expertise in a discipline, researcher-developed learning progressions are empirically derived from research about how expertise develops in a domain. Progression developers begin with a hypothesized version of how expertise develops and conduct empirical research, investigating longitudinal or cross-sectional data from clinical interviews, observations, and assessments to determine the extent to which their hypothesis holds up in reality. Based on the results of these investigations, they make refinements to the progressions and continue with an iterative validation process until a satisfactory representation of students' actual development is reached. A personal communication from ecologist Laurel Hartley to science education expert Charles Anderson nicely captured the process as analogous to an ecological model:

> The steps seem very much the same in that: 1) you start with some initial information and you create a framework or model that you think is an accurate representation of how things really are; 2) then you make predictions based on your model and you "ground-truth" [or validate] those predictions by seeing if what your model predicts is what happens in actuality; 3) then you use that new information about how well your model worked to further refine the parameters of your model; 4) then you ground-truth and adjust parameters again and again until your model becomes a satisfactory representation of reality.[18]

Third, common to most views on learning progressions is that they should identify learning performances, or descriptions of what kind of tasks students at a particular level on the progression are able to perform. For example, mathematics education expert Jere Confrey provided a description of what to expect when students have reached level two of a progression outlining the development of children's mathematical understanding of equipartitioning, which involves the coordination of three essential understandings: 1) creating the correct number of groups, 2) creating equal-sized groups or parts, and 3) exhausting the whole or the collection.

> Once children can coordinate the criteria, some use benchmark fractions (e.g., halves or fourths) to create parts to allocate, though often this strategy leaves remaining parts to share for which children may or may not be successful. For example, when sharing among three, a student may make four equal-sized parts, allocate one part to each sharer, and then be unable to share the remaining piece fairly. At the highest level of proficiency, students create the correct number of equal-sized parts and exhaust the whole using parallel, sequential cuts on rectangles or radial cuts on circles.[19]

In addition, Jere Confrey helpfully provided a description of what performances to expect when children work toward level two, along with examples from individual students.

> When young children begin working on level two, they are often unsuccessful at coordinating the three equipartitioning criteria. They may create multiple unequal-sized parts by "chopping" the whole into many pieces and allocating them. Others create the correct number of parts, but the parts are of unequal size. Some students create equal-sized parts but create too many of them and want to "throw away" the extra parts. Each approach reflects children's efforts to integrate the three requirements into a scheme for equipartitioning a whole.[20]

As this example suggests, the development of a learning achievement frequently involves the integration of several elements, any one of which may lag behind the others. The teacher's use of learning progressions correspondingly involves determining which elements may need additional attention and support in order to facilitate the full integration that will constitute the ultimate learning achievement.

Fourth, progressions many not necessarily be linear. Even within a domain, the constraints and affordances of different types of knowledge will interact to change students' trajectories. For example, knowledge of a particular science concept and the students' abilities to use it will be influenced by their understanding of science practices, such as arguing and reasoning from evidence; similarly, students' abilities to read involve the successful simultaneous coordination of many cognitive and linguistic abilities.[21] So rather than a step-by-step linear representation, a fully developed progression may reflect more of a network, multiple interacting sequences indicating likely relationships between and among various related dimensions that each impact the learning of the others.[22]

Finally, there is general agreement that there is not one definitive path that students follow on the journey toward increasing expertise. At any given point a student may display performances simultaneously at different levels of the progression, a likely artifact of the assessment context and the individual's developing cognition.[23] However, researchers do take the view that it is possible to identify productive pathways that, when combined with effective instruction, can benefit the development of learning in a domain. This perspective is somewhat reminiscent of Dewey's prescient view expressed in 1902:

> the map . . . gives direction; it facilitates control; it economizes effort, preventing useless wandering, and pointing out the paths which lead most quickly and most certainly to a desired result. Through the map every new traveler may get for his own journey the benefits of the results of others' explorations without the waste of energy and loss of time involved in their wanderings—wanderings which he himself would be obliged to repeat were it not for just the assistance of the objective and generalized record of their performances.[24]

Knowledge of learning progressions is a fundamental mapping resource as teachers navigate the contingent terrain of student learning. At the same time, though not a direct resource for students, elements of the map may nonetheless inform the tenor and direction of student learning.

LEARNING PROGRESSIONS AND FORMATIVE ASSESSMENT

Let us recall that formative assessment involves teachers generating and using evidence from a range of sources—including dialogue, observation, and student work products—to inform teaching and learning during its course. This practice requires teachers to be clear about what is to be learned during a more or less extended sequence of instruction. The intended learning goal will ideally, and as often as possible, represent a step on the path toward expertise in relation to an idea or skill in a subject matter area, and be connected to what came before and what will come next. These connections will assist students to develop a "cognitive map" of where they have come from and where they are headed. This cognitive guide is infinitely preferable to students' all-too-common experience of learning as a set of disconnected topics.[25] Teachers also have to specify what a successful performance of achieving the learning goal would be—what the students would say, do, make, or write so that they can create tasks that provide the necessary information to keep student learning moving forward.[26] When teachers have evidence of learning, they can interpret this evidence to determine what it indicates about the status of student learning relative to the intended learning goal. Then they decide on pedagogical responses to propel learning. Progressions can serve as the blueprint for these practices in a number of respects.

With learning progressions, teachers can identify important learning goals and recognize them as part of a bigger story in the development of expertise. For example, from the progression for matter and the atomic-molecular theory a teacher could identify the learning goal of understanding that "objects have certain properties (weight, length, and area) that can be described, compared and measured."[27] She could see that this builds on the idea that "objects are made of different kinds of materials" and develops further along the progression into the notion "that there can be invisible pieces of matter, too small to see." In consequence, the teacher is able to view current learning against a bigger picture of development. In terms of instruction, this view can provide her with the opportunity to build explicit connections between stages in the development of the big idea as students weave increasingly complex forms of the big idea together.

With clarity that the intended learning is focused on the idea that "objects have properties that can be explained and measured," the same teacher has a basis for determining what a good performance looks like and how information about this performance can be elicited. For example, in a classification task the students should be able to accurately sort objects according to weight and area, explain their classification system, and articulate why they have put specific objects in one category rather than another. The task will provide the teacher with information about students' understanding of the goal and enable her to support learning while it develops. For example, the teacher might provide specific feedback to the students, such as "There are three objects that belong in this category and one that doesn't. Look again, think about your explanations, and see if you can figure out which one does not belong and why."

Similarly, using the length measurement learning trajectory, a teacher could identify the learning goal of understanding that fewer larger units will be required to measure an object's length.[28] This is connected to a prior stage of the idea of linear measurement that lengths can "be composed as repetitions of shorter lengths" laid end to end, and a future stage of "possessing an 'internal' measurement tool, mentally moving along an object, segmenting it and counting the segments." She could plan instruction to support the development of students' understanding, for example, "measure in different-sized units for the same object and describe the inverse variations to the length of the unit." This instructional task could also serve as an assessment task by the teacher observing the students' actions and probing their explanations so as to gain insights into their thinking. The teacher would know that a successful performance would be to lay the units end-to-end and to have the students describe the inverse relationship due to the length of the object being measured and the unit of measurement: the shorter the unit of measurement, the more units will be required to measure the object.

The information the teacher derives from this instructional/assessment task while students are in the process of learning can be interpreted against the success criteria. Interpretation of students' various attempts at this task may reveal that some students have a fragmentary understanding, or even an unstable grasp of the idea, or that they are moving toward a stable understanding. In each case, the teacher can decide on the appropriate pedagogical action that will move students to a new cognitive state on the way to meeting the goal.

A further advantage to using progressions is that student learning can be located on a continuum of developing expertise. Mapping formative assessment to a progression of learning can reveal gaps in student understanding that are related to a prior stage in the progression. Perhaps students have not yet acquired the necessary learning on which the current intended learning is dependent. If so, teachers can make the necessary instructional response to fill the gap and enable students to progress. Similarly, if some students quickly reach the intended learning goal, the progression helps teachers to know what is next and move their learning on to a different level. In both cases, the progression allows teachers to make an appropriate match between instruction and the learner's needs. As noted earlier, connecting the instructional experience to the student's current level of learning is a fundamental objective and outcome of formative assessment practice. It is also integral to a children's rights perspective on assessment, which stresses the importance of opportunities to learn, progress, and succeed being offered to children equally.

Despite the benefits that progressions offer to teaching and formative assessment, the current reality is that very few validated progressions actually exist. At present, teachers primarily depend on standards, and curricula derived from those standards to provide them with the basis for instruction and formative assessment. There are inherent limitations in standards for this purpose. In the next section, we contrast standards and progressions to illuminate the limitations.

LEARNING PROGRESSIONS AND STANDARDS

What are the primary differences between progressions and standards as descriptions of learning? First, most standards, including the Common Core State Standards (CCSS), specify the learning expectations that students are supposed to reach at the end of specific grade levels—grade 1, grade 2, and so on—or for clusters of grade levels, grades 1 to 3, grades 4 to 6. These standards are mainly aspirational in the sense that they indicate some societal agreement about what students ought to know and be able to do by the end of specific grade levels.

Second, while standards may represent a coherent progression of aspirations wherein one grade-level expectation is connected to, and builds on, the previous one, they do not trace the pathways, the intermediate steps on the way to meeting the specified grade-level landmark performances. This is problematic for the purpose of teaching because it gives little guidance for the day-to-day practice of formative assessment. In consequence, standards leave teachers with the job of infilling the intermediate steps between one standard and the next. In contrast, learning progressions provide a pathway that serves as a foundation for instruction and formative assessment.

Third, implicit in standards conceived of as end-of-grade expectations is the view that student learning will proceed in lockstep. Indeed, in the case of the CCSS, which are intended as pathways to college and career readiness, if students are not meeting the expectations at the end of each grade, they are not on track to be college and career ready by the end of grade 12. While learning progressions may indicate approximate ages or grades in which student thinking or skills, as a result of effective instruction, will likely transition from one stage to a more sophisticated one, they do not specify grade-level expectations in the way that standards do. It is important to note that the learning performances described in progressions do not represent a set of expectations, but rather indicate the characteristic dimensions of thinking at each stage of the progression.

Fourth, most standards are not derived from research-based hypotheses about how students actually develop concepts and skills in a domain, which then undergo a process of iterative validation as progressions do. In a departure from how most standards are developed, the CCSS mathematics standards are constructed from an assembly of narrative documents that describe the progression of a topic across a number of grade levels and is informed both by research on children's cognitive development and by the logical structure of mathematics, which were then "sliced" into grade levels.[29] However, despite an initial validation process of review by a committee of experts, these standards have not, to date, been subjected to empirical validation studies.

In sum, standards do not provide detailed descriptions of what meeting a specific standard represents in terms of student learning; whereas, learning progressions describe in words, examples, and levels of performance what it means to acquire expertise at each stage of development in relation to the core ideas, principles, or skills of a subject area. A typical example of how standards describe performance is evident in the California Health Standards: to show learning of essential concepts in the Personal and Community Health Standards, students are variously required to "identify the ways to prevent the transmission of communicable diseases," "identify emergency situations," and "describe symptoms of some common health problems and illnesses."[30] Not only do these performances fail to describe what it means to learn concepts of personal and community health, they likely leave teachers scratching their heads about what kind of instruction students need, let alone formative ways to assess where students are in relation to developing understanding. Statements that begin with "identify" lead teachers to superficial summative tasks, by the implicit suggestion that students can either identify ways to prevent the transmission of communicable diseases or they cannot. Such dichotomies are inimical to the development and implementation of formative assessment practices. One consequence can be that teachers end up with the "got it or didn't get it, and then reteach" perspective, which we will discuss more fully in chapter 4. This mind-set is grossly inconsistent with contemporary views of learning where, as we saw in the introduction, theories of the zone of proximal development and scaffolding are key.

For teachers who are left with standards as their guide, basic questions are: What would students be able to do, make, say, or write that shows they have met the standard, and what are the performances that define where students are on their way to meeting the standard? These are questions that are mostly left unanswered; although at the time of writing, in a welcome change from most standards documents, and akin to progressions, descriptions of how student thinking develops within and across standards are being developed to accompany the CCSS mathematics standards.[31]

The development of learning progressions is an emerging field, and while it will eventually most likely yield the corpus of progressions that are needed for teachers across the board to plan instruction and implement formative assessment, teachers cannot wait for the field to catch up. With the limitations of standards and the absence of an extensive set of progressions across subject areas, what are teachers to do? One possible avenue is for teachers to create their own progressions. The next section considers how teachers can develop progressions for purposes of instruction and formative assessment.

TEACHER-DEVELOPED PROGRESSIONS

The development of progressions that span students' entire schooling experience may present an unrealistic and unmanageable task for teachers, especially when they need progressions that provide them with sufficient detail to plan instruction and formative assessment. To make the task feasible, teachers might construct progressions for shorter ranges, possibly to cover likely development across a few grades. Covering more than one grade will also help them address the range of development that is likely present among a class of students. In districts where the work of developing progressions is coordinated and involves groups of teachers addressing the shorter spans that they are most familiar with, bringing the progressions groups together for review and refinement would be a way to create progressions for the entire range of schooling.

See appendix for a set of guidelines that teachers can use to develop their own progressions. These guidelines are represented as series of steps and draw from

Laurel Hartley's ecological model described earlier in the chapter.[32] The best way for teachers to implement these steps is in the context of a group of colleagues—experience suggests it is much more difficult for teachers to do this work alone. It is also useful to either have content experts as part of the group, or have access to content experts to provide guidance and input to the process.

Although time-consuming, teacher-developed progressions can provide the necessary foundation for planning learning and for interpreting and responding to formative assessment evidence. If teachers start by focusing on some core ideas in their subject areas, then over time they can build up their own corpus of progressions. The benefits of developing progressions for teachers are concisely expressed by middle-school social-studies teacher Jason Riley who said developing and using progressions "has changed the way I think about how I plan instruction and how I use formative assessment."[33]

There is also the added payoff that teachers involved in developing progressions engage in a deep investigation of a domain and increase their knowledge about how learning develops in their subject area. This can only expand their ability to promote learning in their classrooms and to engage in formative assessment. For example, when teachers acquire an understanding of how students might represent key ideas in more or less sophisticated ways while developing a progression, they can better engage in interpretive listening (discussed in chapter 1) during the course of ongoing teaching and learning, and can make real-time decisions about what to do next. For instance, they can determine if a student's response means he just needs a little assistance restating an idea or if it indicates a fundamental confusion and then make an appropriate pedagogical response.

Coda to the Guidelines

If the steps of these guidelines appear daunting, to support their use of formative assessment teachers could begin by filling in the intermediate steps that lead from the expectations of one standard to another. In other words, they could decide on the goal-level building blocks that will assist students to move incrementally from understanding and skills represented in one standard to the understanding and skills in subsequent ones. For example, for the CCSS English Language Arts Standards, teachers in an elementary school could lay out intermediate steps between the three standards as shown below in figure 2.1.

FIGURE 2.1

Goal-Level Building Block for Grades 4–6 CCSS Reading Standards

	GRADE 4	GRADE 5	GRADE 6
Standards	INFORMATIONAL TEXT (KEY IDEAS AND DETAILS-RI4.2): Determine the main idea of a text and explain how it is supported by key details; summarize the text.	INFORMATIONAL TEXT (KEY IDEAS AND DETAILS-RI5.2): Determine two or more main ideas of a text and explain how they are supported by key details; summarize the text.	INFORMATIONAL TEXT (KEY IDEAS AND DETAILS-RI6.2): Determine a central idea of a text and how it is conveyed through particular details; provide a summary of the text distinct from personal opinions or judgments.
Understanding	• The main idea is not always stated directly and can be implied in the text • Implied ideas can be drawn from facts, reasons, or examples that give hints about the main idea • A summary is a brief statement that condenses the information contained in a larger chunk of information • Good readers can summarize text as they read	• A text can contain more than one main idea • Multiple ideas in a text can be integrated • Integrating multiple ideas can show the significance of the ideas as a whole	• Extended text can have a central idea (chapters, entire book) • Particular details of the text convey the central idea • Text structure and text features can assist readers to identify the central idea • Summarizing main ideas requires readers to stand back from what they read and view the text objectively • Personal opinions and judgments are different from objective statements
Skills	• Explain how the author implies the main idea (message) in text (1–2 paragraphs) • Distinguish between important and less important details in the text related to the author's message • Explain why some details are more important to the main idea than others • Tell or write a brief statement in student's own words that explains what the paragraph(s) is (are) about	• Describe the main idea of each paragraph (several paragraphs) • Distinguish between important and less important details in the text related to each main idea • Write a brief statement in student's own words integrating multiple main ideas to identify the significance of the ideas as a whole	• Use text structure and text features to signal the central idea of a text • Describe the specific details within the text that convey the central idea • Distinguish fact from opinion in the text • Write a summary in student's own words without personal opinion or judgments that conveys the central idea of the text

Although not the ideal, development of the intermediate steps between grade-level expectations will provide teachers with the opportunity to think carefully about what is required to keep learning moving forward from one standard to the next. This kind of thinking will enable them to determine the goals of instruction, and also to plan formative assessment tasks. For example, when students learn that there is a difference between personal opinion and factual statements, they could engage in instructional/assessment tasks such as underlining facts and circling opinions in a given text and providing explanations of their reasons for the classification. This task could be undertaken in groups, followed by groups sharing, discussing their reasoning, and coming to a consensus. The teacher could listen to their explanations, ask questions to probe their thinking, and with evidence of their current learning status provide instructional adjustments or feedback to move them forward.

When teachers either use existing progressions, develop their own as outlined in the guidelines, or fill in the intermediate steps between standards, they will, to a greater or lesser degree, have the intellectual and collegial support they need to engage in formative assessment practice; they will have productive pathways for student learning as well as the opportunity to align curriculum, instruction, and formative assessment. Above all, they will be able to respond to the individual needs of students, wherever their learning lies on a continuum, and make sure that the best interests of students are taken into account, which as we have discussed is a fundamental attribute of a children's rights approach to assessment.

In the next chapter, we look in detail at how teachers can gather evidence in formative assessment.

Guidelines for Developing Learning Progressions

STEP 1: Start with some initial information and create a framework or model that you think is an accurate representation of how things really are.

The initial information to begin the process of development can be drawn from a range of sources.

- Research syntheses on how learning develops in the domain
- National documents in the subject area
- The CCSS
- Combined professional knowledge and experience about how learning develops
- Curricular guides

From a review of a range of sources, decide on the important ideas or skills of the domain. Once these have been determined, select one or more and, with reference to the information sources, begin with the most rudimentary forms of understanding and identify the successive cognitive moves that students are likely to make as they progress through increasingly sophisticated levels of thinking. These will form the building blocks of the progression.

> **Hint:** *Based on teachers' experience in developing progressions, at this point the level of detail or granularity of the progression could still be an open question. Further discussions may be necessary in the development process to come to conclusions about grain size.*

Next, decide how the progression will be represented. Remember, progressions are not necessarily linear and can take other forms, a web or network, for example. Quite often progressions interact with each other. If a more complete picture is to be developed, a representation showing the relationships between and among different, but complementary, strands of the domain may be preferable. Once the representation is determined, lay out the identified building blocks and discuss the connections between and among until there is an agreed-upon initial representation.

> **Hint:** *Teachers who have engaged in the process of progression development have found it useful to use sticky notes to write each of the building blocks on so that they could move around the sequence as ideas were discussed in the group*

STEP 2: Validate the framework or model.

With a preliminary representation of how learning these ideas or skills develops in the specific domain, the process of validation begins. The first step of the process is to review the progression, addressing the following questions:

- Are the major building blocks in the learning progression addressed?
- Do the building blocks make apparent the cognitive moves across the progression?
- Do these moves make sense in terms of the demands to move from one cognitive state to another?
- Overall, is this a realistic representation, based on the knowledge we have so far, about how students learn this concept or skill in this domain?

Use the responses to these questions to make refinements to the initial model.

Next, give the progression to teachers and other people who have expertise in the domain for review. These reviewers should address the same questions as above, and their responses provide feedback to modify the progression further. At this point, the progression represents "a prediction of what will happen in actuality."*

---

*Laurel Hartley, personal communication to Charles W. Anderson, February 14, 2008, quoted in Charles W. Anderson, "Conceptual and Empirical Validation of Learning Progressions— Response to 'Learning Progressions: Supporting Instruction and Formative Assessment'" (presentation to the Consortium for Policy Research in Education Conference, Philadelphia, PA, February 2008).

STEP 3: Test those predictions by seeing if what your model predicts is what happens in actuality.

Once a "defensible" progression* has been established, the next step is to investigate whether the learning progression happens in reality. There are two ways to do this. First, conduct student *think-alouds*, which involves designing tasks for students that are linked to the building blocks of the progression. For example, if one of the building blocks in the development of analyzing literary text in the middle grades is to have students analyze plot elements and structure, then design tasks to engage students in this analysis. Also determine how students working toward this level will perform on the task, what kind of antecedent understandings will be needed, how students who have reached this level will perform, and how students who have made the next cognitive move in analyzing literary text will perform. Ask a range of students to share their process and thinking when completing the task. Analyze their responses to examine what specific understanding and intellectual processes students actually used to respond. Then, compare the results of the analysis to the progression to determine if what was predicted was what actually happened.

Second, plan and implement instruction based on the progression.

Hint: *Teachers who have been involved in implementing progressions have often found that extant curriculum materials do not serve the progression well. In such instances, the teachers have created instructional materials and approaches that better support students to make the cognitive moves identified in the progression.*

Using the experiences of the different teachers implementing the progression, analyze whether the predicted progression still holds. For example, answer questions such as, when addressing a specific building block in instruction were the antecedent understandings of the progression the ones that were needed to help students make the transition to the cognitive state that is the focus of instruction? Or, was it clear in student learning that the understanding they were developing

---

* James Popham, "The Lowdown on Learning Progressions," *Education Leadership* 64, no. 7 (2007): 83–84.

related to this specific building block was a prerequisite for the next or related stage of the progression?

STEP 4: Use that new information about how well your model worked to further refine the parameters of your model.

Use the information from the think-alouds and the analysis of the implementation of the progression in instruction to refine the progression and bring it closer to what happened in reality.

STEP 5: Validate and adjust parameters again and again until your model becomes a satisfactory representation of reality.

The development of a satisfactory representation is an iterative process. Keep the implementation of the progression under constant review, periodically coming together (across more than one year of implementation) to discuss how learning actually happened and the degree to which the progression represents it. Make refinements after each review until the group is satisfied that "this is the way things are."

CHAPTER 3

Gathering Evidence

Gathering evidence to reveal students' current learning status is one of the signature pedagogies of formative assessment introduced in chapter 1. During the ongoing course of teaching and learning, teachers find ways to elicit responses from students that provide them with the information they need in order to support further learning.[1] This practice reflects the inquiry aspect of formative assessment referenced in this book's title. The evidence teachers gather should help them look "downstream at what can be learned" so as to anticipate future possibilities in learning, enabling them to provide the "just right" kind of support required by students to mature the understanding and skills that are on the cusp of development.[2] Taking this kind of action, as also noted in this book's title, is the counterpart to inquiry.

Over eighty years ago, Dewey pointed the way to evidence collection in support of learning when he observed that what is required for this purpose is "a much more highly skilled kind of observation than is needed to note the results of mechanically applied tests."[3] Such skilled observation by teachers can occur only when students have the opportunity to provide evidence of their learning status through four main types of observable actions: what they say, write, make, or do.[4] These behaviors act as indicators of an underlying learning construct, and are the means through which learning can be inferred by the teacher. Whatever the source of the evidence, the teacher's role is to construct or devise ways to elicit responses from students that reveal their current learning status.[5]

The focus of this chapter is on how teachers can provide students with the opportunities to show their learning status through these four types of observable actions while teaching and learning are underway. We begin with a consideration of specific criteria that teachers should attend to in order to assure that the evidence can be used in support of learning. This is followed by an examination of how one teacher plans for evidence-gathering strategies. Then we review a range of sources that teachers can draw from to gather evidence of learning. Finally, we consider the knowledge and skills teachers need to effectively gather evidence in formative assessment.

THE "FORMATIVITY" OF EVIDENCE

To be formative, evidence must inform teaching and learning during its ongoing course. This idea is encapsulated in a term coined by Frederick Erickson: the "formativity" of evidence.[6] In this section, we examine five fundamental criteria that the evidence a teacher collects about student learning should meet. These criteria are 1) alignment, 2) tractability, 3) universalism, 4) timing, and 5) sufficiency. When the evidence meets all five criteria, then what Erickson referred to as "threats to the formativity" of evidence are minimized.

> **Alignment:** The first criterion is alignment between the success criteria—the indicators the teachers have established for successful performance—and the evidence collection methods they employ. For example, if one of the indicators is that students will be able to explain how Abraham Lincoln in his Second Inaugural Address unfolds his examination of the ideas that led to the Civil War, then a central evidence-gathering strategy will be to elicit oral or written explanations. Similarly, an indicator that students will be able to interpret and mathematize a problem requires an evidence-gathering strategy that involves students in developing a model to translate goals from a written text into a mathematical representation in order to solve the problem and arrive at a correct solution.[7] An important point here is that while the evidence can be in the form of what students say, do, make, or write, the choice of form will be dictated by the success criteria.

> **Tractability:** The second criterion refers to what the evidence reveals that makes it possible for teachers to shape subsequent pedagogical action.[8] For example,

the type of questioning reflected in the Initiation–Response–Evaluation (IRE) or "recitation" paradigm, in which the teacher asks a question, a student is selected to answer and the teacher makes an evaluation of the response, is unlikely to yield productive, tractable evidence.[9] The outcome of this kind of questioning is not to make student thinking visible but rather to let the students know whether their responses are right or wrong, which tends to end the exchange and prevents further dialogue, rendering the information instructionally intractable.[10] Questions that are targeted to reveal specific misconceptions, or that enable students to provide accounts of their thinking, or promote an expanded exchange between teacher and students are more likely to generate information that teachers can act on to advance learning.[11]

Well-designed instructional tasks can also serve as windows into students' learning, permitting teachers to interpret and respond to ongoing events as they unfold during instruction. For example, teachers may act on their observations of how students make changes in their investigation of variables in science, or how they read scales, draw graphs, and use number grids in mathematics (or in other words, what students do).[12] And if teachers use probing questions during their observations to dig deeper into students' thinking, they have additional evidence to use.

Universalism: The third criterion concerns the distribution of opportunities for students to show where they are in their learning. Simply put, the children's rights approach to formative assessment means that all students must be afforded the chance to move forward from where they are currently. As we know, students do not move in lockstep as they learn. In any classroom, the students will be at different points in their learning during a lesson and teachers will need to take account of this when deciding how they will collect evidence. It will be important to ensure that whatever means are selected will capture a range of possible levels of understanding and skills within each student, as well as for all the students in the class, so that each one will have the chance to display his current learning status. Without this, opportunities for formatively guided pedagogy may be lost, and the chances for progress of individual students will be diminished. Open-ended tasks, discussion, or questioning practices are more likely to secure responses that are indicative of each student's learning status than the kind of closed questioning characterizing the recitation paradigm discussed earlier.

Timing: If evidence is to have maximal value in informing next steps, it needs to be proximate to learning so that teachers can take immediate or near-immediate action. According to Paul Black and colleagues, formative assessment can be planned into the rhythm of instruction so as to become an organic feature of pedagogy and of the students' learning experience.[13] For example, it may be that during the course of a lesson there are certain points when the teacher needs to make sure that students understand some foundational aspects of a new concept before they can continue to develop the ideas. Evidence gathering around these points can be planned into the instructional sequence, or they may arise spontaneously as a component of the learning process. The teacher may also decide that toward the end of the lesson he wants to give students an opportunity to show their current understanding of the concept, and asks for a quick written response to a question designed to reveal their understanding, which he can use to plan the subsequent lesson.

Sufficiency: The final criterion concerns the sufficiency of information to make a decision about appropriate pedagogical action. Teachers have to answer the question, "Do I have enough information here to make a reasonable decision about this student with regard to this domain of information?"[14] In practice, this might mean a teacher has evidence from a student representation, from observations of the student constructing the representation, and from probing questions about the nature of the representation—why the student constructed it in a particular way and what it means. In other words, observing the student construct the representation may not have provided sufficient evidence, but in combination with what the student said the teacher has sufficient information to make a decision. Only when the teacher is satisfied that there is enough information about the student's learning will the formative value of the evidence be assured.[15]

Gathering evidence that meets these five criteria involves a process of planning in advance of instruction. In the next section, we will examine how teachers can plan for systematic evidence gathering.

PLANNING FOR EVIDENCE GATHERING

In an example taken from Roderick Thompson, a science teacher from Catalina Foothills School District, Arizona, we can see a range of ways in which he plans to elicit evidence of learning as a lesson comprising three ninety-minute periods unfolds.

Figure 3.1 shows the overarching big idea in science that frames the lesson: DNA is a warehouse of the genetic code that provides information that controls cellular structure. He has also included cross-cutting concepts from the Next Generation Science Standards (NGSS) that he thinks apply well to the structure of DNA, and, additionally, he plans to focus on the Common Core State Standards, English language arts (CCSS ELA) for science grades 6–12 reading and writing. Mr. Thompson has also specified a learning goal for the lesson derived from the big idea: Understand how the *structure* of DNA *relates* to its function, as well as the prior knowledge that students will have to begin this lesson.

Figure 3.2 describes the success criteria that Mr. Thompson will communicate incrementally to the students as the lesson develops. These serve as indicators of

FIGURE 3.1.
Formative Assessment Planning

BIG IDEAS:
- DNA is a warehouse of the genetic code that provides information that controls cellular structure and activities.
- NGSS framework dimension 2, Crosscutting Concepts, number 6, Structure and Function.
- CCSS ELA for science grades 6–12, reading and writing.

PRIOR KNOWLEDGE:
Proteins are macromolecules made of specific sequences of amino acids (structure). Proteins have many functions that control cellular structure and activities.

LEARNING GOAL:
By the end of the lesson students will understand how the structure of DNA relates to its function.

TIME:
Three blocks of 90 minutes.

FIGURE 3.2

Formative Assessment Planning

Success Criteria: Can I . . .	Formative Assessment Strategies
Define the terms structure and function?	*Questioning:* Whole class. Teacher describes EITHER a <u>structure</u> OR a <u>function</u> of familiar objects (e.g., a chair) and students write an S or F on their whiteboards. Select students to explain response—do others agree/disagree and why?
Describe the structure of DNA?	*Draw/Label:* Individual/pairs. Students label various diagrams of DNA. *Make:* Students make a paper model of DNA. *Say:* Students describe to each other their drawings, models, and observations of an animation using the correct vocabulary.
Explain why the base pair rule means DNA forms complementary strands and a double helix?	*Questioning*: Individual while pairs are making and labeling DNA model. 1) Explain why A and T bases form a complementary pair <u>BUT</u> A and C do not? 2) How does the base pair rule explain that DNA forms complementary strands? 3) Why does DNA then form a double helix?
Demonstrate the process of transcription?	*Make/model:* Pairs. Students use a set of manipulatives (or smart board) to model how DNA is transcribed into RNA. Use sample of pairs to present models/class discussion. *Note:* Essential to check for accuracy.
Use a codon chart to select correct amino acids given the RNS codon triplet?	*Questioning:* Whole class. Read out an RNA codon triplet and students write amino acid equivalent on their whiteboards. Repeat several times. Generate discussion and summarize key points.
Demonstrate the process of translation?	*Make/model:* Pairs. Students use a set of manipulatives (or smart board) to model how RNA is translated into a polypeptide/protein. Sample pairs present models/class discussion. *Note:* Essential to check for accuracy.
Use a DNA sequence (structure) to construct a polypeptide/protein (function)?	*Questioning/make/model*: Individual/pairs. Students work through a set of scaffolded questions and tasks that provide practice for transcription and translation. The final task is to generate the correct DNA base sequence of a complementary strand from a short polypeptide. Explain why it is correct.
Explain how a mutation (change in DNA base sequence) may or may not alter the function of a protein?	*Questioning/writing:* Individuals. Students write a paragraph explaining how changing the base sequence of DNA <u>may</u> or <u>may not</u> cause a functional change. Ask each student: 1) How might a change of one base in the DNA sequence change the amino acid sequence in a polypeptide? 2) How could this affect the cell structure or activity? 3) Can you explain why a change in the DNA base sequence might NOT alter a cell's structure or activity?
Read about a mutation and summarize the content referring to the structure and function of the DNA and how they are related?	*Draw:* Individual. Students draw and label the DNA sequence, described in the text, in the unmutated and mutated form. Students write a summary, using textual information, explaining how the two types of DNA produce different functions in a cell. (Relating structure of DNA mutation to its 'new' function.)

progress that both he and the students will use throughout the lesson. He has carefully constructed the criteria so that they align with the learning goals. The success criteria are written in a way that students can understand and are also framed as questions to support students to use them as an internal guide of their own learning. Next to each criterion Mr. Thompson has included the strategies that he will use in his lesson to generate evidence about his students' learning.

We can review Mr. Thompson's formative assessment strategies in terms of the five key criteria for formativity.

First, the strategies are clearly aligned to the success criteria he has specified. For example, a criterion is that students will be able to explain why the base pair rule means DNA forms complementary strands and a double helix, and he plans to use an evidence gathering strategy that requires students to provide an explanation. Similarly, another criterion is that students will be able to demonstrate the process of transcription, and for this his evidence-gathering strategy is to engage students in making models of how DNA is transcribed into RNA and to ask students to explain their models. Second, the nature of the tasks Mr. Thompson asks students to engage in—providing oral explanations, making models, and drawing and labeling diagrams—meets the criterion of universalism. They are sufficiently broad to capture the range of learning among the class. Third, they are likely to yield information that is instructionally tractable: they will produce sufficient evidence of the students' learning status to enable Mr. Thompson to make any needed pedagogical adjustments at levels ranging from the individual to the whole class, and from tweaks to wholesale changes. Fourth, the strategies are fully embedded into the projected lesson activities, so they will almost certainly meet the proximate timing criterion: Mr. Thompson will discover issues to be addressed on a "just in time" basis. Finally, in terms of the sufficiency criterion, Mr. Thompson has used multiple strategies to pursue student understanding. For example, the criterion use a DNA sequence (structure) to construct a polypeptide/protein (function) requires students to make models in pairs, to work through a series of scaffolded tasks, and to generate a DNA sequence as a proof procedure of their understanding, all in the context of responding to Mr. Thompson's ongoing questions.

In figure 3.3, we can see that he has identified possible misconceptions that he can be alert for during the lesson, and take steps to probe for them during his questioning. He has also identified specific vocabulary that he will expect students

FIGURE 3.3
Additional Planning Notes

POSSIBLE MISCONCEPTIONS/CONFUSIONS:

- Mix up structure and function terms.
- Make complementary strands parallel rather than anti-parallel.
- Mix up base pair rule.
- Confusion about why A and T are complementary but not A and C.
- Difficulty using the RNA triplet codon chart.
- Using T instead of U in RNA, Using U instead of T in DNA, transcribing T to U not A.
- All mutations are BAD!!
- All mutations cause a change in the protein structure.

VOCABULARY:

Structure, function, double helix, anti-parallel, complementary, base rungs, sugar/phosphate sides, H-Bonds, transcription, translation, codons, RNA, A, C, T, G, U, anti-codon, ribosome, polypeptide, mutation.

OTHER QUESTIONS
(extension, higher-order thinking, etc.):

1) What do you think are some of the pros and cons of cells having DNA in the form of a double helix rather than a single strand?
2) What do you think are some of the pros and cons of cells having DNA in the nucleus rather than loose in the cytoplasm?
3) What are some of the evolutionary inferences you could hypothesize about DNA based on its structure?

to use and will listen and look for in their oral and written explanations. To make sure that he has the questions that can both lead to and probe higher-level thinking ready when he needs them, Mr. Thompson has noted three that he will use during the lesson.

As Mr. Thompson's lesson plan vividly illustrates, when teachers plan instruction, they also need to plan to opportunities for evidence gathering during the lesson. Of course, this does not mean that formative evidence cannot arise spontaneously during the lesson—it can. But the point here is that evidence gathering should not be left to chance. Otherwise evidence gathering may not serve the core purpose in formative assessment for which it is intended.

In the next section, we move from teacher planning to an examination of a teacher's interactive evidence gathering practices in real time.

TEACHER–STUDENT INTERACTION AS FORMATIVE EVIDENCE

Interaction between teacher and students has been characterized as a principal source of evidence in formative assessment.[16] Indeed, Black and Wiliam suggested that interactive dialogue is at the heart of formative practice.[17] In a further elaboration, Allal and Pelgrims Ducrey observed that interactive formative assessment is intended to provide scaffolding in the student's zone of proximal development (ZPD), the place where Vygotsky hypothesized that learning takes place.[18] The following vignette presents an analysis of teacher–student interaction in which the teacher uses her interactions with individual students as a source of evidence. In addition, we see evidence gathering integrated with pedagogy.[19]

There are thirty students in Ms. Castaneda's third-grade class. In this lesson, the students are working on writing expressions with parentheses and are given a word problem on the board, which they are to solve using expressions with parentheses.

Expressions with Parentheses

Nia earned $11 for pulling weeds and $10 for cleaning windows. She spent $7 on a movie ticket and $3 for snacks. She saved the rest of the money. How much money did Nia save?

Ms. Castaneda preconstructs the task with the whole class using three steps to solve the problem in the following sequence, which eventuates in the students stating that they need to identify the question, the clues, and keywords for response (sequences of interaction are verbatim transcriptions of video footage of the lesson):

Ms. C: I want you to discuss what do we need to know in order to solve this problem? And there are three steps. Who can remember one of the three steps to solve this problem? Daniel?

ST1: Identify a question.

Ms. C: Okay. Then we identify a question.

ST2: We identify the clues.

Ms. C: Okay. Then we identify the clues. Umm, go ahead.

ST3: Look for keywords.

Ms. C: And keywords. Okay. I want you all to turn to your partner and I want you to identify all three. The questions, the clues—remember there might be more than just one—and the keywords. Now go ahead and discuss that together.

The students then move to work in pairs to solve the problem. Students in this class are accustomed to working both collaboratively and independently. While the students discuss the problem with their partners, Ms. Castaneda moves around the pairs and explores their progress. This is a routine practice in her math class and includes one-on-one conversations with each student while the second student listens in. When Ms. Castaneda reaches Rico and his partner, she begins with a question designed to identify Rico's initial approach to the problem:

Ms. C: And what was your first step in solving this problem?

Rico: First is to underline questions, clues, and keywords [he has used different color highlights].

Ms. C: Okay.

Rico: (Pointing at paper) These are the questions and the key words and the clues.

Ms. C: So, can you go over with me some of the key words you found in this problem?

Rico: I found that she earned, spent, saved, and . . .

Ms. C: So there were several keywords. There wasn't just one keyword in particular right?

Rico has also made a representation of how he solved the problem using expressions with parentheses. He has solved the problem correctly. At this point in their interaction, Ms. Castaneda asks Rico to explain the thinking behind his solution—in essence, how the language of the problem was translated into a mathematical expression:

Ms. C: Now I noticed that you went a step further and you tried to solve this problem (points at paper). Now I also noticed that you used an expression rather than an equation. Can you—how did you do this? Can you show me how you came to that conclusion of using that expression?

Rico: Well, like, she earned 11 for pulling weeds and 10 for cleaning windows; so if she earned them so I added them because it said that she spent 7 dollars on a movie ticket and 3 for a snack, so I used the math to do this because then I get confused. So I—instead I added the ones that she earned and added the ones that she spent it on, and just to show that—just so I won't get mixed up, I put parentheses because to learn that, umm, that I am going to subtract them.

Ms. C: So I see—so you put parentheses around the 11 and the 10, then you put parentheses around 7 plus 3. Right?

Rico: Yes.

Ms. Castaneda's awkwardly phrased question: "Can you show me how you came to that conclusion of using that expression" is apparently designed to avert a focus on the answer, in favor of how he arrived at the representation, which is her target of interest. Her question invites an extended explanation of Rico's thinking, in which he shows that he first adds items labeled "earned" and also items labeled "spent" before going on to subtract the latter from the former. His observations are elaborated by numerous pointing gestures to the marks on his notebook. He also explains that he used the parentheses to remember which items fell in which categories.

Ms. Castaneda continues the conversation by exploring Rico's next step after putting the numbers in the parentheses:

Ms. C: Now what's your next step after putting parentheses around?

Rico: To add what's in the—in the open parenthesis and the closed, what's inside of it. I have to add it.

Ms. C: So, your first step was going to be to solve what's inside the parenthesis. Okay. Why don't you go ahead and show us what you came up with.

Rico: I came up with 21 with the 11 plus 10, and 10 is the 7 plus 3, and then since I figured out that the minus was still there (points to the minus between the parentheses), so I put it there (points to the minus between the numerals 21 and 10), and I did 21 minus 10, which gave me 11.

Ms. C: And eleven—is that your final answer?

Rico: Eleven dollars (adds dollar sign to his result).

In this exchange, Ms. Castaneda focused on Rico's understanding of the need to solve the operation expressed in each parenthesis prior to any subsequent step.

Finding his understanding to be solid verbally (as well as representationally) she proceeds to his final step in the problem—subtracting the money spent from the money earned. At the conclusion of the interaction, Ms. Castaneda tests Rico's commitment to his final answer to the problem. Rico's confirmatory response—accomplished via repetition, rather than a simple "yes"—assumes complete ownership of the solution, and he underscores this ownership by simultaneously adding a dollar sign to his circled, written answer.[20] Before she leaves Rico and turns to his partner (who has been intently listening to their exchange), Ms. Castaneda asks Rico to share his strategy to the whole class during the final plenary session of the lesson. Students sharing strategies is a routine practice in her class at the end of a lesson. Then she records the substance of her interaction in her notebook and also her judgment that she needs to plan for a further extension of Rico's understanding before the next lesson.

In the sequence just described, we see Ms. Castaneda operationalizing the five criteria for quality evidence. The evidence she elicits is aligned to the success criteria, setting up the problem as an expression with parentheses, solving the problem, and providing an explanation of how the strategy worked, it is proximate to Rico's learning and provides her with tractable information that she can use to plan his next steps. She clearly meets the criteria of sufficiency of information with her use of multiple sources of evidence. Before this interaction, she already has two sources of evidence from his notebook: his highlighted elements of the clues and keywords for response, and his representation of a solution to the problem. However, she decides to probe the thinking that led to the representation. She does this through open-ended questions that permit Rico to establish the sequencing of his thinking and, at each next step, enable him to determine the way forward. The result is that her questioning, though sequentialized in terms of the problem-solving pattern, is one that allows the nature of Rico's thinking to emerge with only minimal scaffolding. In the process, Ms. Castaneda becomes sure that Rico grasps the whole problem, including translating the language of the question into the language of mathematics, and the logical series of steps required to solve the problem.

One-on-one conferences, as Ms. Castaneda and her students refer to the interactions, are a hallmark of evidence gathering in her classroom. These evidence-gathering conferences do not occur ad hoc. Before each lesson, she determines which students will be the focus of the conference time, which occurs when students work independently, either individually, in pairs, or in small groups. After each conference she makes notes in her file about what has ensued. In addition, she uses student work products, her observations of how they approach the classroom tasks, and classroom discussions to decide which students she needs to confer with each day. The conferences are one of the routinized participant structures in her classroom. The students know what is expected of them during the conference and they know that each one of them will have the opportunity to interact with their teacher so that she can understand where they are in their learning. Ms. Castaneda is clear that the conferences are an essential resource for her to inquire into students' learning status so she can keep each one on track to meet desired goals.

Mr. Thompson's and Ms. Castaneda's evidence-gathering practices embrace the principles of a children's rights approach to assessment. To enact the principle of all children being served equally well by their assessment practices, the teachers systematically provide opportunities for each individual student to display the nature and quality of her thinking. Without this systematic provision, the teachers would not be able to make the proximate decisions to foster progress in the best interests of each child. In terms of the principle that no subgroup of students should be adversely impacted by assessment practices, because these teachers make a point of consistently inquiring into the nature and status of their students' learning, and take informed action intended to move each student's learning forward, the risk of some students being adversely impacted diminishes.

In the evidence-gathering examples from Mr. Thompson and Ms. Castaneda, we have observed a range of sources of evidence. Among these are one-on-one interactions with students, teacher observation, whole-class questioning, class discussions, students' explanations generated from white board responses, and students' work products, including math problem solving, models, written work, and labeled diagrams. Note that none of these sources is a "test" or an "assessment" per se. Instead, the sources arise from the lesson context so that evidence gathering is seamlessly integrated into teaching and learning. In this vein, it is useful to be reminded that, in their now-famous 1998 review, Paul Black and Dylan Wiliam referred to assessment in the context of formative assessment as all the activities undertaken by teachers and by the students through self-assessment that provide information to be used as feedback to modify the teaching and learning activities in which they are engaged.[21] They make clear that formative assessment is neither a specific test nor a specific instrument. This is not to say that an instrument cannot be used as for formative assessment—it can—provided it meets the criteria outlined earlier in this chapter. It is worth noting here that many of the ubiquitous online item banks proffered to teachers as resources for formative assessment in fact more closely resemble interim or summative assessment items, and may be less than effective as resources to generate insights into student learning as it is developing. "Caveat emptor" (or buyer beware) was the core of assessment expert Lorrie Shepard's conclusion when commenting on these commercially available item banks in 2005, and this advice remains salient at the time of writing.[22]

In addition to those discussed so far, there are other sources of evidence available to teachers that they can plan to use in the context of ongoing teaching and learning. Some of these sources are briefly reviewed in the next section.

OTHER SOURCES OF EVIDENCE

In the area of reading, Bailey and Heritage offered a range of strategies to gain information about students' reading, including students reading texts aloud, strategic questions focused on the text, and prompted written responses about text as ways to elicit evidence about students' learning.[23] Specifically in the context of science curricula, but relevant to other areas, are what Shavelson and colleagues, referred to as "embedded-in-the-curriculum" formative assessment.[24] These are specific assessment tasks placed in the ongoing curriculum by teachers or curriculum developers at key junctures in a series of lessons. Key junctures are points in a learning sequence (e.g., understanding the concept of relative density) at which students need to consolidate certain understandings before moving on to the next level of sophistication in the sequence. The embedded assessment opportunities provide teachers with information they can use to determine whether the students are ready to move on or if they need further assistance to consolidate their understanding.

Technology offers some promising ways to support evidence gathering. For example, the online program Agile Assessment enables secondary school teachers to construct a range of cognitively demanding assessments to assess higher-order thinking in mathematics.[25] A web-based tool, Strategic Reader, designed for use with struggling middle school readers, provides a flexible assessment and instruction environment so that teachers can gather evidence of student performance during the instructional episodes and employ interventions as needed for individual students.[26]

Finally, Dylan Wiliam suggested fifty techniques for eliciting evidence.[27] These include extended wait time for responses to higher-order questions, students' ranking examples of other students' work, and students' using ABCD cards to respond to multiple-choice questions, which are designed to reveal potential errors or misconceptions students might have about a topic.[28]

Whatever the source of evidence teachers decide to use, they will need to know about the criteria for the formativity of the evidence and attend to them when they are planning how they will gather evidence. Doing so will help teachers obtain the evidence they need to keep student learning moving forward. In addition to knowledge about the criteria, there is a range of other knowledge and skills that enable teachers to gather evidence of student learning. These are considered in the following section.

TEACHER KNOWLEDGE AND SKILLS FOR GATHERING EVIDENCE

The knowledge and skills exhibited by Mr. Thompson and Ms. Castaneda were not acquired either quickly or automatically. Both teachers are committed to the value of formative assessment to their students' learning and have spent, and continue to spend, time and effort to develop their knowledge and skills for evidence gathering.

Successful evidence gathering is dependent on clarity about what is to be learned. In other words, teachers need to be clear about the intended learning in any instructional sequence—not what the students will do, but what they will learn as a result of their classroom experiences. A major strength of the teaching exemplified in this chapter is that both teachers focus on the specific learning goals for the lesson that they have created. Once teachers have identified the learning focus, the next step is to decide what the criteria are for successful learning: what students will say, do, make, or write that indicates they have met the intended goal. Mr. Thompson's lesson plan describes the success criteria he will use, and in the interactional sequence with Rico Ms. Castaneda's evidence gathering is clearly targeted at specific indicators.

Being clear about the learning goal and the success criteria is dependent on subject content knowledge, as well as on knowledge of how students learn within the specific subject area. In the conception of learning as one of increasing expertise described in chapter 2, the identified learning goal is connected to prior learning and to what will come next, so that it is part of a bigger learning arc. Experience shows that when teachers have limited content knowledge and limited knowledge of learning in the subject area, they can have difficulty establishing learning goals that are connected to what came before and to what follows, and in specifying success criteria matched to the goal. In such cases, the temptation may be to resort to what students will do in the lesson, for example, make a model of DNA or solve word problems, as opposed to establishing first what the students will learn from doing these activities. Establishing what the students will learn provides answers to why they are making a model or solving problems and helps teachers decide if these are the best activities to reach the intended learning goal. When teachers are clear about the focus of the learning, then they can better decide on the indicators that will signal progress, the success criteria.

With clear learning goals and success criteria teachers select the method or strategy they will use to gather evidence in the course of ongoing instruction. As we have seen in this chapter, there are various ways to gain insights into a student's learning status. Whatever way the teacher decides to collect evidence, as this chapter has stressed, it should meet the criteria for formativity. So teachers need both knowledge of these criteria and the knowledge of a range of evidence-gathering approaches. In addition, teachers need the skills to select a particular method that will meet the criteria in a specific learning situation.

In cases where teachers and students are engaged in the give and take of interactions, teachers will have to simultaneously invoke and operationalize subject matter knowledge together with knowledge of the success criteria as they probe students' current learning status in situ. Both subject matter knowledge and criteria knowledge will be necessary to guide their interactional practices so that they acquire the evidence they need.

In contrast to standardized assessment, the locus of control in formative assessment practice rests with teachers. They determine how and when to gather evidence and they also determine whom and what to assess. In some instances, the teacher might want to have evidence at a particular point in an instructional sequence from all students so he might pose a question, ask students to respond on a white board, which they then hold up for the teacher and for each other to see.

This could become an opportunity for further probing if some students are asked to explain their response, as Mr. Thompson had planned to do in his lesson. In other circumstances, a teacher might want to work with a small group of students during a lesson to discuss their problem-solving strategies and gain insights into their thinking. Or, as in the vignettes, teachers might plan individual one-on-one time with specific students in a lesson to ascertain their current learning status. The ability of teachers to engage in these diverse practices will be dependent on their classroom management skills and the degree to which a community of practice has been established. In classrooms where students understand their responsibilities as learners and are able to be resources for one another, teachers will be more easily able to engage in evidence gathering that reveals where students are in their learning. For example, in Ms. Castaneda's classroom, students have already come to understand the importance of their one-one-one time with the teacher and have learned to be sufficiently independent to manage their own learning or, when needed, to seek the assistance of their peers. Of course, this is because the expectations have been clearly set out by the teacher, the classroom is organized so that students can be independent and access materials and resources they need, including each other, and the students have had ample opportunity to practice becoming more responsible for their learning.

Successful evidence gathering is not dependent on one single aspect of teacher knowledge and skills. Instead, teachers bring together in a coordinated way the knowledge and skills discussed here to ensure they have the information they need, when they need it, in order to advance each student's learning.

In the next chapter we will see how teachers use the evidence they have elicited to meet the learning needs of all their students.

CHAPTER 4

Interpreting and Using Evidence

I n an excerpt from an interview about formative assessment, a third-grade teacher from Syracuse City School District, New York, introduces the focus of this chapter by describing how she uses evidence in support of student learning.

> I could look at [the students' problem-solving strategies] and see that not all kids were struggling in the same area. I could use that piece of information and see specifically what kids were struggling in, what area to intervene on—what they needed instead of reteaching everyone and working, you know, in a whole group setting, and kids who already knew it, or they didn't have that misconception, they weren't getting retaught it . . . or [I wasn't] teaching something that they didn't need and then it was a quick fix. You know they could meet in small groups, you could meet one-on-one, or you could even have a peer teach them if you had to, but [you can use] that piece to guide your instruction.[1]

From her description, we learn that she interprets the evidence she gathered in the course of the lesson to determine individual students' needs with respect to their understanding of the problem-solving task, and then she provides assistance, utilizing different grouping strategies, that led to a "quick fix" for each student. This chapter develops the ideas introduced by the teacher from Syracuse. First, we consider the zone of proximal development (ZPD) as the "just right gap." Next is a discussion section on interpreting evidence, which is followed by an examination of targeted assistance to students. The chapter ends with a consideration of the knowledge and skills teachers need to use evidence effectively.

THE JUST RIGHT GAP

In his seminal article, D. Royce Sadler conceptualized formative assessment as a feedback loop designed to close the "gap" between students' current learning status and desired goals.[2] Sadler stressed that the gap will vary from student to student. Invoking the story of Goldilocks as a metaphor, the central point of interpreting and using evidence is to establish the just right gap for each student, a growth point in learning that involves a next step that is neither too large nor too small. In the applied context of the classroom, the notion of the just right gap is another way to think about Vygotsky's idea of the zone of proximal development. Used in this way, the just right gap points to the difference between the learner's current accomplishment on an individual level and what the learner can reasonably be expected to achieve with appropriate external assistance or support.[3] When teachers interpret evidence and decide on the subsequent appropriate intervention, they make determinations about the distance between what the learner can accomplish independently and what can be accomplished with their assistance.[4] As Vygotsky famously observed, "What the child can do with assistance today she will be able to do by herself tomorrow."[5]

Identifying the just right gap is the core of the children's rights approach to assessment, because it is the direct incarnation of the principle that opportunities to learn, progress, and succeed will be offered to children equally. If students' learning opportunities are not matched to their current learning levels, then some children will be at a disadvantage because the tasks that are proffered and the experiences that come from these tasks are too easy for them, while others will find the material too hard. In both situations, the students are not served well by their teachers and are not afforded equal opportunities to progress.

The first step for teachers in identifying the gap is to interpret the evidence they gather while teaching and learning are underway. In the following section, we will look closely at what is involved in evidence interpretation.

INTERPRETING EVIDENCE

In formative assessment teachers interpret evidence on an ongoing basis. Successfully interpreting evidence depends on teachers' knowledge of the subject matter, which encompasses what Jerome Bruner called the "structure of knowledge"—the theories, principles, and concepts of a particular discipline.[6] In addition to the structure of knowledge, teachers also need knowledge about how student learning develops in the subject, for example, what learning looks like when it is emergent or in the midst of change as students take steps to develop their understanding and skills from the prior level they have reached to a new, more advanced level. And teachers also need to know what indicators will show when students have reached the desired performance—what students will be able to say, write, make, or do.

In this example from a high-school English as a Second Language (ESL) classroom, we can observe a teacher who has both subject matter knowledge and knowledge of what emergent learning looks like.

> The teacher has created a five-week unit on linguistics with the purpose of guiding his students through a deep exploration of an academic theme, while at the same time placing a focus on the language needed to express their ideas. So far, the students have formulated questions they would like to explore about language, and have researched a variety of sources on the topic. As an assessment task, the teacher asks them to write a letter to someone they are acquainted with, telling them what they have learned so far about language. Before the lesson is over, five students write their beginnings on large sheets of paper that are shown to the class to prompt a discussion on what they have done so far and where they need to go to next. An animated conversation develops about whether animals have language or not. Julio, not part of the five initial volunteers, decides to read his letter aloud to the class.
>
>> **Julio:** First of all, I think that language is a way to inform others around you, your feelings or just a simple thing that you want to let know people what is the deal. And it can be expressed by saying it, watching a picture, or hearing it, you know what I'm saying? I don't know if you have heard about the kangaroo rat that stamps its feet to communicate with other rats. It's really funny 'cause we humans have more characteristics to communicate to each other, but we still have problems to understand other people. Characteristics like sound, grammar, pitch, and body language are some of them, while the rat only uses the foot (he stamps the ground).
>
> From Julio's reading, the teacher determines that Julio has some initial understandings about the nature of language and decides that he will assist Julio to develop his ideas on the characteristics of language. In terms of Julio's academic language skills, the teacher notes that he is mixing registers, using language such as "you know what I'm saying" in the context of what is intended to be the more formal register of a letter. Assisting Julio to understand the idea of register will be the teacher's next step for him in terms of academic language development.[7]

Julio's teacher is able to make a determination about Julio's academic language and writing development because his subject matter knowledge provides him with a clear conception of what constitutes fully formed understanding and skills in the context of this task. Importantly, he is aware of what such learning looks like on the cusp of development. The teacher has the skills to decide what to do next to support Julio's learning. He has generated and interpreted evidence about the ZPD, the bandwidth of competence that currently exists and which Julio can navigate with assistance to move to a more advanced state of competence.[8] In this way, the teacher works on the edge of Julio's learning, discussed in the introduction, to close the gap.

An example from Jim Minstrell, an expert in science assessment, and colleagues underscores the importance of subject matter knowledge and interpretive skills in the context of physics lessons on the relationship between force and motion.

> In explaining horizontal motion, highly skilled interpretation by teachers noted that the inexperienced physics students typically expressed speed as proportional to the net force acting on the object. Thus, when the object was speeding up the net force was getting larger and larger and when the object was moving with constant velocity the net force was constant. Meanwhile, these teachers also pointed out that at least the students were likely correctly distinguishing between constant speed and speeding up. Teachers with lower levels of interpretation tended only to note that the students were wrong about the net force needed and recited the correct relation between force and motion.[9]

In this example, we see two different interpretations that will lead to different responses, one that is more likely than the other to lead to deeper learning. Teachers that are highly skilled in interpreting evidence are able to identify learning that is emerging and make a judgment about the gap between where the students are in their understanding of force and motion and a more fully formed understanding toward the desired goal. Their assistance can be contingent on the students' responses, targeted to build on what the students already know and lead them incrementally to a more developed understanding of the relation between force and motion. In contrast, the lower-skilled interpretation, which is concerned with correctness rather than on what aspects of the concept students do understand, leaves teachers with only one judgment to make about the gap—students are still on the starting blocks with respect to achieving the desired goal. Students in these classrooms are in one of two categories: those who understand and those who do not. The teachers' response is to provide the students with the correct information about the relation between force and motion and, in so doing, short-circuits students' opportunities to really understand the relationship. In this vein, we are reminded of Piaget's advice that "each time one prematurely teaches a child something he could have discovered for himself, that child is kept from inventing it and consequently from understanding it completely."[10] In the above example, learning about force and motion is not left to the students to "discover" for themselves. Careful assistance that builds on the level students have reached supports them so as to arrive at an appropriate understanding in their own way.

Learning progressions that include descriptions of developmental levels for each stage in the progression can help teachers make determinations about the status of student thinking or skills. For example, returning to the trajectory for equipartitioning described in chapter 2, a teacher's interpretation of evidence may reveal that students are at the beginning point of coordinating three essential understandings (creating the correct number of groups, creating equal-sized groups or parts, and exhausting the whole or the collection): they are able to share a whole into the correct number of parts, but the parts are of unequal size. The teacher's action then can focus on providing the necessary assistance to move the students to a new cognitive state where they understand that parts they create from the whole need to be of equal size.

Similarly, a progression that describes the development of expertise in social studies writing can help teachers interpret different levels of performance among their students.[11] For example, evidence may show that students are maturing their skills with respect to text cohesion: they are including more developed causal language (e.g., *for this reason, therefore*), transitional expressions (e.g., *also, in addition, similarly*) are present, even if not always used appropriately, and there is mostly a thematic progression, an idea referenced at the end of one sentence begins the next. In this case, the teacher can target assistance on fine-tuning students' use of transitional expressions and their understanding of thematic progressions to bring their skills to a more secure, consolidated level.

Without knowledge of what constitutes a fully formed understanding or skill as well as the intermediate states of learning, teachers are limited in their ability to interpret the evidence they have obtained and determine current levels of student learning, identify the just right gap, and take appropriate action. The more progressions with descriptions of intermediate levels, as in the equipartitioning and social studies example that the teachers have, the better they will be able to determine how students' learning is developing and know what to do next.

In the next section, we consider in more detail the assistance teachers can provide to close the gap between where the students are currently in their learning and the intended learning goals.

TARGETED ASSISTANCE

There are two main forms of assistance that teachers can provide in response to their interpretations of evidence: scaffolding and feedback to students.

Scaffolding

Scaffolding is a metaphoric concept used to describe the assistance provided by adults and peers that enables learners to solve a problem, carry out a task, or achieve a goal that would be beyond their unassisted efforts. The necessity for scaffolding is a key indicator that learning is taking place, because it is only then that learning is being undertaken within the student's ZPD.[12]

According to Wood, Bruner, and Ross, scaffolding involves a range of functions. These include the following: enlisting the student's interest in and adherence to the requirements of the task; reducing the number of steps required to solve a problem by simplifying the task; accentuating certain features of the task that are relevant; keeping the student "in the field" to pursue the particular objective by making it worthwhile for him or her to risk the next step; controlling frustration; and demonstrating or modeling an idealized version of the task.[13]

Scaffolding also has three other important properties:

1. It is contingent. For scaffolding to occur, the teacher uses strategies that are clearly based on immediate and contemporary student responses.
2. Scaffolding should fade, in that it decreases over time, at a rate dependent on the student's rate of acquisition and competence.
3. Scaffolding involves transference of responsibility from teacher to student, in which the responsibility for performance, in particular, is gradually handed over to the learner.[14]

For example, a child learning the component sounds of words might not yet be able to isolate the sounds. As a scaffold the child is shown pennies to represent each sound in a word as the word is sounded out (e.g., three pennies for the three sounds in "man"), then is asked to place a penny on the table to show each sound in a word. Finally the child is asked to sound out the word without the pennies.[15] The coins provide a contingent scaffold to help the child move from assisted to unassisted performance of the task. In a high school science class, a teacher might provide assistance to students by first giving them detailed guides to carrying out experiments, then giving them brief outlines to structure experiments, and finally asking them to design experiments entirely on their own.[16] The guidelines and outlines provide the scaffolds to move students to the successful performance of independently structured experiments. In both examples, the task is simplified, relevant features of the task are accentuated, and, as in the second example, idealized, and frustration is controlled.

The term scaffolding is frequently used synonymously with instruction in the sense of a teacher-initiated, directive instructional strategy. This kind of strategy is evident when a teacher implements a lesson comprised of small, sequenced tasks that all students undertake simultaneously under a teacher's direction. This usage is in conflict with the original metaphor, which stresses responsive assistance to the immediate configuration of student needs "in the moment."[17] Since teacher-initiated, directive instruction lacks the characteristics of contingency, decreasing levels of assistance and transfer of responsibility, it remains methodologically different from scaffolding. While a lesson in which formative assessment occurs may begin with teacher-initiated, directive instructional strategy, teachers' responses to students as a result of gathering and interpreting formative assessment evidence will be contingent on what the evidence shows about their learning.

To Wood and colleagues' conceptualization of scaffolding, Roland Tharp and Ronald Gallimore added instructing, questioning, and cognitive structuring.[18] Instructing involves an explanation of how something should be done and why; questioning entails asking students questions that require an active linguistic and cognitive response; and when cognitive structuring is the intention of scaffolding, the teacher provides "explanatory and belief structures that organize and justify."[19] In the vignette that follows, we can see these elements of scaffolding at work.

In Ms. Butler's fifth-grade class, her twenty-seven students are learning about persuasive writing. Their topic focus is on "what people can do to improve the environment." In previous lessons, students learned about the idea of "arguments" (the proposition that the student is advancing) and "reasons" to support the argument, which Ms. Butler framed as "all the reasons why people should listen to me." In this lesson, the students have focused on counterarguments. Ms. Butler has worked through an example on the white board, using a graphic organizer labeled into three sections: arguments, counterarguments, and reasons/opinions. The students have the same graphic organizer in their notebooks and are at different stages in developing arguments, counterarguments, and reasons. During the students' independent writing time Ms. Butler joins Joshua with a request that he share with her what he is working on (this is a verbatim transcription from a video recording).

Ms. B: Okay, so, what are we working on right now?

Joshua: Um, I'm looking for my reasons (Joshua points at his arguments on paper), and then sometimes when I find more reasons I, like, get more counter arguments and I look for more reasons and I get more the counter arguments.

Ms. B: So, you've already thought (Ms. Butler points at Joshua's written argument) about some counterarguments and now you are working on adding more reasons (Ms. Butler points at Joshua's written argument) to support . . .

Joshua: The argument and then sometimes when I get some of these, I get more counterarguments, so I keep on adding more.

Ms. B: (Ms. Butler nods) So, it gives you more ideas right? So the more reasons you have . . . the more ideas you get for counterarguments. So it's good to be prepared. That's the point of developing these kinds of arguments because having these counterarguments (Ms. Butler points out the arguments on paper) will help you to make a stronger argument for yourself because you are thinking ahead and you are thinking about what are people going to say that is going to be against my . . . what I believe. So, that's right! Can you read me your argument?

In this exchange, Ms. Butler's questioning elicits sufficient evidence of Joshua's progress, and the assessment process has proceeded to the point that Joshua is willing and able to complete her sentences in a collaborative meeting of minds.[20] As is clear from these exchanges, Joshua is progressing well, and Ms. Butler has satisfied herself that he understands the concepts of "reasons," "argument," and "counterargument" and is deploying these concepts productively in his planning graphic.

From when Ms. Butler says "So it gives you more ideas, right?" onward, she corroborates his understandings and offers an additional reason for thinking through his ideas, pointing to the value of anticipating opposing points of view.

As their exchange continues, Ms. Butler builds on Joshua's discussion of arguments and counterarguments in a process of joint expansion of his understanding.

Ms. B: Okay, and what are some of the reasons why they might not want to be a part of this?

Joshua: Uh, because sometimes people don't care, or they're just like really mad.

Ms. B: And why would you say that?

Joshua: 'Cuz you know how people are really busy sometimes, and sometimes they're like concentrating on their work more than other stuff that are happening so they like, like, put them to the side and work on what they are going to work on, like their work.

Ms. B: That's right. (Ms. Butler nods) So, do you think there are some people that don't believe in global warming?

Joshua: Yeah, they're like some people that really need to recycle and waste lots of stuff.

Ms. B: They waste things, so do you think there are people who don't believe there is anything wrong with not recycling?

Joshua: Yeah.

Ms. B: And do you think that could be another counterargument?

Joshua: (Joshua nods) Uh huh.

Ms. B: That they just don't believe that there is anything wrong or that they don't believe that there is anything happening to the earth.

Joshua: Mm hm. (Joshua slightly nods) Or like, they just like, look up in the sky and it seems normal, so they just say the world is normal and they don't care about the global warming.

Ms. B: . . . And, everything's fine, right? (Ms. Butler nods while speaking)

Joshua: Uh huh.

Ms. B: And there's nothing wrong. That could be a major point that you might have to contend with later on. Some people might say, I don't believe in global warming. I don't believe that this is something that is affecting the earth or affecting me, so that's going be something that you are really going to have to think about, and think about counter arguments for that, okay? So, I'm going leave you with that thought. Think about that, and think about what you would say to them to counteract, to counter argue that point. Okay?

Ms. Butler's first question in this excerpt is about why some people might not want to join the fight against global warming. Joshua's initial response adds relatively little that would be useful in the context of argument and counterargument, and Ms. Butler presses him a little: "and why would you say that?" Joshua responds that people are distracted by their own work and other preoccupations. Joshua's responses convey no more than that, contrary to the self-evident existence and significance of global warming, there are people who are too busy, preoccupied, or "mad" to pay proper attention to the problem. At this point Ms. Butler introduces an additional consideration that takes Joshua's thinking a step further: people's preoccupation and indifference to global warming, the focus of his argument, may border on outright disbelief. Apparently, this idea does not immediately resonate with Joshua who perseveres with the idea that these people should be recycling, but without registering or embracing the notion that the failure to recycle may be associated with disbelief in global warming. In response, Ms. Butler acknowledges his point, but then reconfigures her previous question to focus on whether there are people who do not really believe in recycling. Gaining his assent, she further scaffolds this line of reasoning into the possibility that such people do not believe in global warming itself (the question she had previously asked). It is at this point that Joshua has a moment of creative breakthrough: "Or like, they just like, look up in the sky and it seems normal, so they just say the world is normal . . . " This imaginative leap is conjoined with Ms. Butler's suggestions with the connective "or," thus offering, from Joshua's point of view, a third alternative.

In this example, the teacher's scaffolding contributions are, after a little hesitation, directly built upon by the student in a process of assisted coconstruction. Joshua's final contribution is constructed as an addition to the teacher's thinking at both the linguistic level (via the connective) and at the conceptual level through its recognition of the incremental nature of climate change as a fundamental factor impeding the general acknowledgement of global warming. The teacher's process of contingent scaffolding is instrumental in advancing Joshua's thinking.

Feedback to Students

As we have seen, interpreting evidence involves making a determination about the existing discrepancy between the actual and the desired state of students' learning. When teachers provide either oral or written feedback to students about their learning, they give the students information about this discrepancy with advice on action they can take to reduce it.

When feedback is effective it can serve a scaffolding function. However, researchers have shown that not all feedback is effective. For example, feedback that is interpreted as critical, focused on the person rather than the task, or that compares a student's performance with his peers can have negative effects on learning.[21] In addition, if the feedback is too long or too complex, students will likely not pay attention, which renders it useless.[22] What kind of feedback can serve as a scaffold and be effective in supporting learning?

A meta-analysis conducted by Avraham Kluger and Angelo DeNisi showed that feedback that focuses on providing information about how the student performs a task and gives suggestions that can be taken up by the student about how to improve is much more effective than evaluative feedback that only informs the student how well she is doing.[23] This finding has been confirmed in other studies.[24] Similarly, in a historical review on feedback, Raymond Kulhavy and William Stock[25] reported that effective feedback provides the learner with two categories of information: verification and elaboration. Verification indicates a judgment about the correctness of the answer and elaboration provides information that guides the learner toward the correct response.

In the example that follows, during a one-on-one conversation, an elementary school teacher provides oral feedback that both verifies student learning and elaborates on it to help the student improve her written work.

Teacher: Now your second paragraph here really makes some excellent connections. So you're talking about the reasons that you chose the longhouse to draw and you're talking about your ancestors and you also related it to the PowerPoint presentation that you did in class a couple weeks ago. So

> that's fantastic, I think you've made some great connections. Did you want to tell me about any of those connections that you made?

Student: In my connections, why I related it to my ancestors because, in our PowerPoint, mine was on the Northeast Woodlands Iroquois tribe and the Northeast Woodlands is where we live now so that really could have been where our ancestors first, like, lived and had any histories to do with the first nation's people.

Teacher: That's excellent. So your first two paragraphs were fantastic. Now looking at your third paragraph, I don't think it's quite on topic, you're supposed to be writing—if we look back over here (teacher points to the page)—at the how, describing the steps that you took to create this piece. So I think you got a little off topic in that third paragraph and you're still doing some relating it to yourself. So if you want to include that part—in the second paragraph—and then rewrite your third paragraph stating the steps that you took to actually draw that particular piece. Okay? So I'll write that down for you.[26]

In her first response, the teacher indicates where the student has been successful and invites her to discuss the connections she has made to herself in her writing. In her second response, the teacher indicates a discrepancy between the current work and the desired performance, and provides the student with a suggestion about how to move closer to the desired performance. With the suggestion teacher provided, the student is able to rework her third paragraph to describe the "how."

Feedback as a scaffold can also be provided in the context of a class discussion, as we see in the following example where middle school students are engaged in a discussion about legal and moral rules.

Teacher: Is it wrong to steal?

Jane: Depends.

Teacher: Depends on what, Jane?

Jane: It depends on your point of view.

Teacher: Does this mean that right and wrong is only decided by a person's point of view? I mean if everyone thought stealing was morally right, would that make it right?

Jane: Er . . . I'm not sure . . . I suppose so.

Teacher: Sam? You've got your hand up.

Sam: I disagree! I mean if everyone stole things life would be crazy. You wouldn't be able to trust anyone. You wouldn't dare leave home, because all your neighbors would steal your things before you got home. That couldn't ever be right.

Teacher: Good thinking Sam. Can you think of a way of describing your ideas?

Sam: Er . . . common sense I suppose.

Teacher: Okay, but common sense for what purpose? Would people still be able to call themselves a society if they all stole from each other?

Sam: No.

Teacher: Why not?

Sam: Well, society is a bit like being in a team. A team only works if the members work together.

Teacher: Good. I like your metaphor. Society is like a gigantic team of people working together. Experts call Sam's reason, a social reason (puts on board). The social reason says if we are to all live as a society there are certain moral or legal reasons or rules we all have to obey. Otherwise there could be no society. Jane, what do you think of Sam's answer?

Jane: Sounds okay, I suppose.

Teacher: I'm not sure what you are saying. Do you still think that right and wrong are always a matter of opinion or are you saying he is right and there are certain fundamental moral reasons for saying some things are right and some are wrong, whatever a person may say?

Jane: Well I think Sam's answer is right most of the time, but if I lived in a country where there were lots of really, really rich people and my baby was starving to death because I was really poor, I would steal from the rich people to keep my baby alive and I don't think that would be wrong.

Teacher: Wow! I think we have some budding philosophers in this class. Good thinking, Jane. Philosophers would call your idea situation ethics. An American professor gave us a theory of right and wrong called situation ethics (puts on the board). He said, "There's no right and wrong for every situation. He said you have to work out what's right and wrong on the basis of love." Jane, does his idea about love match your idea?

Jane: Yes. Course it does. If you love your baby, keeping that baby alive is more important than taking a bit of food from a really rich guy.

Teacher: Good. Can anyone else think of any situations where it might be the most loving thing to break the normal rules? Yes Emily?

Emily: When we watched that video about Martin Luther King, that woman called Rosa broke the rules about not sitting in a white person's seat. I think she was right to do that.

Teacher: Well remembered. That's another good example. Okay, now let's try to work out why it's usually right to obey legal and moral rules and why it might be morally right sometimes to break rules. James, any ideas?[27]

In the discussion the teacher assesses the students' responses, acknowledging the points students have made, framing supplementary questions as feedback to guide or move their thinking along. The teacher uses praise and explains why the response is worthy of it. Recognizing that Jane's reasoning was vague, the teacher goes back to her so that she could reflect further on her first answer. As a result she extends her own thinking and that of the class. In his final response, the teacher reminds the students of the learning goal.[28]

Oral feedback can also occur within the context of reciprocal teaching strategies: summarizing, questioning, clarifying, and predicting. For example, in a middle-school art lesson students examine the painting *Peasant Wedding* by Pieter Brueghel.[29] The teacher first asks the students to summarize what they think is happening in the painting. In this section of the lesson, teacher feedback could be to note the relevant aspects that the students have included in the summary and to suggest that they "think about what elements in the painting contribute to the idea of a celebration." Then in the questioning part of the lesson where the students are asked to question the artist's choices, after listening to a series of responses the teacher might say "You have done a really good job of asking questions about Brueghel's choice of color and brushstrokes. Now see if you can develop these ideas further and ask questions about their contribution to the mood of the painting." In the clarifying part of the lesson, when the teacher is helping the students clarify details in the painting, feedback might be "So you have noticed that there is a small boy in the right of the painting. Can you clarify what you think he is doing there? Can you describe what he is doing?" During this class discussion in which the teacher provides feedback to individual student responses, peers listen to the feedback as well, which in turn, prompts them to develop their own thinking.

Teachers can also provide feedback in written form as we see in the next example where a high school teacher gives feedback about a student's written response to the task: describe how conflict resolution can build peace in local or global communities.

> You have correctly identified the eight stages in the conflict resolution model. Good job!
>
> Stages 3, 4, 6, 7, and 8 are accompanied with some good description, as required by the task.
>
> You could give a fuller description of all points, especially 1, 2, and 5. Why is it important to respect the person/government with whom you are in conflict? Can you refer to a specific example of where this was necessary and how both sides managed to achieve this?

The teacher has "verified" what the student has done well and has provided a suggestion, an elaboration that serves as a scaffold to assist the student to develop her thinking about conflict resolution.

Of course, written feedback to each student can prove very time-consuming. To reduce the load on teachers in providing written feedback, Shirley Clarke proposed coding systems that can communicate information quickly and easily to students.[30] She also suggested that such coding systems are particularly useful with younger children. An example of a coding system is when the teacher lets the students know how she will annotate their work:

> I will choose three places where you have successfully made me feel how that character was feeling and circle or highlight those bits. I will also choose one place where you could have said more about how one of the characters was feeling and I will put an arrow to show where you could have written more.[31]

In this instance, the teacher can annotate the students' work quickly and the students receive accessible feedback that they can act on. It will be up to the teacher to decide when it is important to spend the time providing written feedback and when coding systems can be effective.

A crucial element of feedback is that it should help students in the process of "mindful" knowledge development.[32] To this end, feedback needs to scaffold learning by providing hints, cues, or suggestions the students can use to close the gap between their current learning and the desired goal. Noteworthy in all the cases discussed earlier in the chapter is that the teachers do not provide the entire solutions to the students. Doing so would foreclose the students' opportunity to use the assistance to engage in the regulation of their own learning. Students' self-regulation will be the focus of the next chapter.

In formative assessment, when teachers interpret evidence they need to provide scaffolding or feedback within an immediate or near-immediate timeframe. Advance or contingent planning can help teachers to take swift and appropriate action in support of learning.

Contingent Planning

Because of the immediacy of teachers' responses in formative assessment, Threlfall proposed the notion of contingent planning.[33] As the name implies, contingent planning involves anticipating the range of responses that students are likely to show, and determining, in advance, what a possible course of action would be in light of specific responses. To anticipate student responses, teachers draw from their knowledge sources, the structure of the discipline and how learning develops within it. By anticipating the likely responses among the students in the class, teachers will be able to plan different paths of action depending on what assessment information reveals about where the students are in their learning.

In another example from Jim Minstrell and colleagues' research, we can see the value of teachers anticipating in advance what students will likely show in their physics explanations:

> In using forces to explain constant velocity motion of a skydiver with the chute open vs. closed, highly skilled teachers identified the central issue, i.e., students tend to think that there needs to be a net force downward proportional to speed. These teachers correctly predict that beginning students will explain constant speed with a constant net force and explain constant acceleration with a constantly increasing net force.[34]

The teachers in this example are in the highly skilled interpretation category and have anticipated how students who are at a beginning stage of understanding will present particular explanations. In so doing, the teachers plan contingent responses that allow them to capitalize on these early understandings. It is easy to imagine that, in these teachers' lessons, the flow of the learning runs without a hitch.

Teachers elicit explanations and, because they have anticipated what will character-ize them, they can act upon them immediately, moving seamlessly between assess-ment and assistance.

Recall Mr. Thompson's planning from chapter 3, which illustrated how he iden-tified a lesson learning goal, success criteria, and strategies to use in the course of the lesson to elicit evidence of the students' learning status. As part of his plan-ning process, Mr. Thompson also thought about how students would demonstrate different states of learning, for example, what they would say, do, make, or write when they were at a beginning stage of understanding of the intended learning goal. During the lesson, this forethought enabled him to interpret evidence and take action in situ. He was able to identify the discrepancy between the students' current levels and desired performance as students revealed their thinking through the assessment strategies he deployed. Furthermore, he decided in advance what kind of assistance he would provide to students who demonstrated each level of the understanding. For example, one of his success criteria was that "students can explain why A and T bases form a complementary pair but A and C do not." In his planning notes he indicated that students with a beginning or emerging under-standing would explain why A and T form a complementary pair but would not yet understand why A and C do not. In this instance, his response would be "to use four cards labeled A, C, G, T with corresponding H-Bonds, either two or three and show the student that only those with 2 H-Bonds would pair (A–T) or only those with 3 (C–G). A with 2 and C with 3 would not 'fit'." With his support, the student would then "practice three or four possible pairs drawn at random from the four EXPLAINING why they paired or not." In terms of scaffolding, Mr. Thompson demonstrated an idealized version of the task and kept the student in the field to pursue the particular objective by making it worthwhile for him to risk the next step. He also faded the scaffolding and transferred responsibility to the student through these practice opportunities.

In another example from the same lesson, Mr. Thompson noted in his plans that students who had not yet fully grasped how the base pair rule explains that DNA forms would likely understand the ladder form but would not yet able to connect it to the relationship with the double helix. One response to this level of understanding would be to "have the student take a paper 'ladder' model and cut it vertically in half, through the H-Bonds and separate the two sides. Place one on top of the other and show the student that although the bases are complementary (A on top of T for example) the sides are not . . . the top and bottom do not exactly line up." In scaffolding the student's learning, Mr. Thompson engaged the student in a simplified task as well as accentuated certain relevant features of the task. Because of his careful planning and thought about how students would manifest different stages of understanding during the process of teaching and learning, Mr. Thompson capitalized on "moments of contingency" as they arise in the classroom.[35] He made pedagogical responses that were contingent upon the students' current learning status, building on what they already knew to move them incrementally through a process of scaffolding from their current state of learning to a more advanced state.[36]

As we noted in chapter 3, while evidence gathering in formative assessment practice is planned, there are times when students will say or do something spontaneously that provides a source of insight into student learning. It is important to note that the kind of contingent planning described in this chapter does not preclude assessment opportunities arising in the course of a lesson. Moreover, by engaging in contingent planning, in the event of spontaneous opportunities, teachers will be better prepared to respond to where students are in their learning than they would in the absence of such planning.

This chapter began with the idea of formative assessment practice as a feedback loop. Throughout this chapter, we reference the knowledge and skills that teachers employ when they determine and scaffold the just right gap. In the chapter's concluding section, we consider some further aspects of the knowledge and skills that will help teachers use evidence effectively.

TEACHER KNOWLEDGE AND SKILLS

Effective formative assessment is a process involving the interpretation of evidence and the provision of scaffolding and feedback. To be effective, this process depends on teachers' recognition that the feedback loop is not a one-time event, but rather a heuristic for teaching and learning. Students begin a period of learning with a gap between what they know and what they are expected to know. They engage in experiences and activities designed by the teacher to assist them to close the gap. In the course of these activities, teachers need the skills to interpret evidence of the students' current learning status to determine the discrepancy between the level of learning the students have reached and the desired performance—this difference representing the just right gap. When a discrepancy exists, teachers need the knowledge and skills to provide scaffolding or feedback that is contingent upon the students' current level with a view to closing the gap. Teachers continue the process of evidence gathering, interpretation, and scaffolding/feedback until students have reached the desired performance and the gap is closed.

When this process is framed within the students' rights approach to assessment, the central point of interpreting evidence is to establish the just right gap for each student. It follows that the key idea in scaffolding and feedback is to respond to individuals in terms of the gap that exists between where each student is as an individual, and where she needs to be so she has the opportunity to progress. Only if the individual student's learning is the focus can opportunities for each child to learn, progress, and succeed be provided.

However, this principle does not mean that teachers are obliged to offer individualized instruction to students on a consistent basis. Not only is this idea impractical, it is also not desirable. Students learn from their experiences and interactions with each other, and this kind of situated learning is a vital feature in the development of each student as a learner. Meeting individual students' learning needs in a situated way requires skills in establishing a well-structured classroom environment. The elements of a well-structured environment include the provision of accessible materials and resources related to the focus of the learning, which allows students to be independent of the teacher. It also includes an organization of physical space that permits different groups and configurations of students so that teachers can adapt their responses to a range of students.

Finally, skills in the signature pedagogies described in chapter 1—routinized and mutually understood practices of behavior and interaction, enabling student agency, and modeling values and attitudes—establish the expectations and routines for how students will learn together and permit the teacher to respond to the range of student learning needs indicated by the interpreted evidence. Ultimately, it is the convergence of the knowledge and skills described here that enables teachers to effectively interpret and use evidence in support of student learning.

In the next chapter, we focus on how students use evidence in support of their own learning.

CHAPTER 5

Learning How to Learn

A core objective of formative assessment is to involve students in the management of their own learning. Involving students in the assessment process is a key component of this objective. Students who participate in the assessment process develop the capacity to reflect on where they are in their learning, to understand where they need to go next, and to work out what steps are needed to get there. To be involved in this way, students need to understand both the desired *outcomes* of their learning and the *processes* of learning through which these outcomes are achieved, and they need to be able to act on this understanding.[1] Just as their teachers engage in a process of inquiry and action, so too do the students. This process can enable students to become active, autonomous learners who take responsibility for their own learning. In short, students need to learn how to learn. Their teachers' role in formative assessment is to help them reach this goal.

Students' acquisition of growing responsibility and autonomy in the learning process will likely become a key, not only to their own futures but also to the future of our society. In 1998, visionary mathematician and computer scientist Seymour Papert described the future in the following terms:

> The model that says learn while you're at school, while you're young, the skills that you will apply during your lifetime is no longer tenable. The skills that you can learn when you're at school will not be applicable. They will be obsolete by the time you get into the workplace and need them, except for one skill. The one really competitive skill is the skill of being able to learn.[2]

In recent years, the idea expressed by Papert, often termed "learning to learn," has become prominent in education policy circles, notably in the European Commission's Centre for Research on Lifelong Learning. As the demands of knowledge economies become increasingly complex, students need not only to learn academic content but also, as the phrase "life-long learning" implies, to develop the resources, capacities, and habits that will enable them to continue learning beyond school and throughout their adult lives.[3]

The findings of the United Kingdom's Learning to Learn Project suggest that learning to learn is not a simple set of activities or techniques.[4] David Hargreaves captured the complexity of what is involved in his working definition: "Learning to learn is not a single entity or skill, but a family of learning practices that enhance one's capacity to learn."[5] To draw attention to the development of students' learning practices—the "how to" of learning—Paul Black and colleagues emphasized "learning *how* to learn." They noted that their focus on the "how to" of learning is consistent with the idea of Assessment for Learning (formative assessment), which they refer to as "a label for a group of practices that have been shown to help pupils improve their learning."[6]

This chapter focuses on the ways that formative assessment contributes to the development of the practices associated with learning how to learn. We begin with a discussion and examples of student reflection and decision-making in learning. We then turn to the idea of metacognitive activity, and follow this with an examination of how teachers can assist their students to develop metacognitive skills. The relationship between metacognition and self-efficacy is considered next. An examination of how peer-assessment can help students develop metacognitive skills follows. The chapter ends with a discussion of the knowledge and skills teachers need to assist students to engage in metacognition to benefit their learning.

LEARNING HOW TO LEARN: STUDENT REFLECTION AND DECISION MAKING

The introduction presented a framing idea for each of the book's chapters: a children's rights approach to assessment. One of the primary components of a children's rights approach is that students should be engaged meaningfully in all aspects of the learning process. The scope of this principle must embrace assessment as a fundamental aspect of student involvement. From this perspective, student engagement means that teachers are not solely responsible for the assessment of their students; instead, students become comparable stakeholders with the right and obligation to play a significant role in analysis and reflection about their own learning, and in decision making about next steps. Developing the practice of reflection and the ability to make judgments and arrive at decisions based on reflection are two skills that enhance students' capacity to learn. In turn, they undergird the notion of personalized learning, discussed in the introduction, because they contribute to the development of learning dispositions, habits, attitudes, and identities that enable students to become lifelong learners.

With this background, let us now consider some examples of classroom practice.

Example A: In Mr. Alvarado's first-grade math class, toward the end of each lesson, the students use their review sheet to reflect on their own learning. Before the lesson concludes, the students take a moment to complete their individual sheets. At the end of the week, each student goes over his or her sheet and completes the final section, "my goal for next week will be to . . ." Figure 5.1 shows how one student in the class filled in his sheet.

During the final math class of the week, Mr. Alvarado meets briefly with each student to discuss his or her goal and together they make a decision about the appropriateness of the goal the student has established. Mostly, the teacher is in agreement with the goals the students have set for themselves.

Example B: The students in Ms. Wilsons's second-grade class use an organizer to set reading goals each day. The organizer, completed by one of the students in his class, is shown in figure 5.2.

At least once during the course of a week, Ms. Wilson has a one-on-one reading conference with each student. At this time, she discusses how well the students met their goals, what steps they took to make sure they were able to meet the goals, and if they didn't meet their goals, what they need to do and what help they think they need.

Example C: A self-reflection tool that Ms. Pernisi, a sixth-grade math teacher, regularly uses in her classroom is an exit ticket on which the success criteria for the lesson are written. Ms. Pernisi makes time in each lesson so that the students can rate themselves against the success criteria for the lesson. Figure 5.3 shows how one student completed an exit ticket for a math lesson on plotting points on all four quadrants.[7]

FIGURE 5.1
Self-Reflection Sheet

Name: *Jalal*

October 27 to November 14, 2011

This week, I did the following in math:

Math topic	Date I did it:	One thing I learned:
Building Numbers	11-8-11	*I learned how to add numbers*
Estimation/Counting	11-8-11	*I learned how to estamate*
Standard Form, Expanded Form, Word Form	11-7-11	*Whow to write nubers*
Comparing Numbers		
Problem Solving	10-27-11 11-3-11	*I learned how to add cookeis* *I learned how to cont betr*

My goal for next week will be to:

Learn how to cont with coins

In the same class, another student rated herself as 5 on all three criteria and for the final section about what she thought she needed more time learning to meet the goal, she wrote "Nothing, I got it all down." And she had! The students know that Ms. Pernisi uses their exit tickets along with the evidence she has from her own assessment strategies to make decisions about next steps in their learning.

Example D: In Mr. Hurst's ninth-grade social studies class, the students keep a reflection/planning log, which they complete each day. In this lesson, the students were investigating what makes an historic event a turning point. Working in pairs, students had identified a specific event that

FIGURE 5.2
Reading Log

Reading Log		
Date: 1-18-12	Title: Mummys in the morning	Pages Read: 23-44
My goals for today as a reader: Is to plan were I am going to read at		
Date: 1-19-12	Title: Mummys in the morning	Pages Read: 44-64
My goals for today as a reader: Is to make pordictoins of whats giong to hapen next		
Date: 1-19-12	Title: Pirates Past Noon	Pages Read: 1-4
My goals for today as a reader: Is to stop when it dose not make seans		
Date: 1-20-12	Title: Pirates Past Noon	Pages Read: 4-12
My goals for today as a reader: Is to talk back to the book with a schema sentens stem		
Date: 1-23-12	Title: Pirates Past Noon	Pages Read: 12-34
My goals for today as a reader: Is to get throw tricky spots		

they were going to research from primary and secondary sources, and then analyzed its historical significance. Figure 5.4 shows how one pair of students completed the log at the end of the lesson.

At the end of each day, Mr. Hurst quickly reviews each log and sometimes adds a suggestion for the students' consideration to deal with a difficulty they have identified. He also uses the information the students provide to decide if he needs to work with specific individuals, or pull a group together for a mini-lesson, or to have a discussion with the whole class.

FIGURE 5.3
Exit Ticket

Think about your learning . . .

Circle the number that you feel best matches your level of success with each item.

I can talk and write about plotting points using correct vocabulary.

Not at All				Absolutely
1	(2)	3	4	5

I can plot points in all four quadrants.

Not at All				Absolutely
1	2	3	(4)	5

I can create a rule for ordered pairs (x, y) for quadrants I, II, III, and IV.

Not at All				Absolutely
1	(2)	3	4	5

After this lesson, I feel like I need more time learning.

Graphing

FIGURE 5.4
Reflection/Planning Log

Reflection/Planning Log

What was successful about your learning today?

We've been successful in taking notes from a primary source we located.

What difficulties or problems did you encounter in your learning?

We encountered difficulties finding other primary sources to assist our research.

How did you manage those difficulties? Were you successful? If not, what plans do you have for dealing with them in the next lesson? Whom do you need help from?

We decided we needed to come up with different key words and subject headings. Tomorrow, we are going to ask David and Jasmine to help us think of a new list and we will try that. If we are not successful, we will most likely ask for your help.

Across these four examples, we see teachers involving students in formative assessment practices that support the skills necessary to learning how to learn. First, the teachers provided tools for the students' reflection. Some of the tools are generic, for example, the reading log, which can be used irrespective of the particular book the students were reading. Others, for example, Ms. Pernisi's math exit ticket, are tailored to the specific lesson. Second, the teachers make time in each lesson for student reflection. This is well expressed by Ms. Pernisi when she was asked to think about changes in practice as a result of developing her skills in formative assessment:

> I used to do more but now I do less. Because so much evidence is gathered with formative assessment, I may do 2 or 3 very targeted tasks in an eighty-minute class rather than 'lots of good stuff.' Now I work hard to save time for student reflection rather than filling every minute with activity.[8]

Third, the teachers help students evaluate their own learning through a variety of structures and routines in each lesson. And fourth, the teachers ask their students to think about future goals in light of their evaluation. In sum, the students both reflect on their learning and take action based on those reflections.

Signature Pedagogies

Let us return briefly to the signature pedagogies of formative assessment discussed in chapter 1 to consider how they can help create the context for student reflection and action. Each of the teachers in the previous examples established routines and mutually understood patterns of behavior in the classroom through which students can participate in the assessment process. The students are supported to become agents in their own learning through these routines and through interactions with their teachers. For example, reflecting on learning is included as part of the established routine of classroom life, and teachers involve their students in discussions about the judgments the students have made about their progress. Through these routines and interactions, in turn, teachers model the values of respect and caring for their students. They take seriously the students' own evaluations and ideas of what they need to do next, and incorporate them into the learning process. Finally, because teachers create the participant structures for students to make judgments about their learning, and because they model the values of respect and caring in the way they treat students' judgments, students see themselves as contributors to the process of assessment. Students understand that it is both their responsibility and that of their teachers to use their respective judgments in reciprocally supportive ways to progress learning.

Engaging in the kind of reflective and action-oriented processes we see in the classroom examples supports students to develop what is referred to in the literature as metacognition and self-regulation processes. These processes are elaborated in the next section.

LEARNING HOW TO LEARN: METACOGNITION AND SELF-REGULATION

Metacognition has been variously described as "relating to the human capacity to be self-reflective, to consider how one thinks and knows"; "cognition that reflects on, monitors or regulates first-order cognition"; and "the ability to reflect on one's performance."[9] Inherent in these three definitions is the idea of students bringing their learning to a conscious level. In so doing, students can gain better control over their own learning.[10] Gaining conscious control over one's learning is an essential dimension of learning how to learn.

Metacognitive activity is generally considered to take the form of an internal dialogue that enables self-monitoring during an activity. For example, competent readers constantly ask themselves if what they are reading is making sense, if they are creating mental pictures, or if they know the meaning of specific words. And when what they read does not make sense, they do not create images, or they do not know what words mean, they have strategies to assist comprehension. Through self-monitoring, they generate internal feedback. They are able to act on this feedback because they have a repertoire of strategies to draw from. So metacognition involves both self-monitoring and self-regulatory action. Self-regulatory action includes the mechanisms of goal setting, planning what to do next, evaluating and revising strategies, determining when to seek assistance, when to persist with an approach, and when to adjust learning strategies.[11] All of these mechanisms are necessary for effective intentional learning.[12] The successful employment of these processes is clearly associated with achievement differences among students.[13]

If we return for a moment to our examples, we can see that students are engaged in developing metacognitive skills, including self-regulation. For instance, the students in Mr. Hurst's history class self-monitored, adjusting their learning strategies, and deciding when they might need help from their teacher. Similarly, the first- and second-grade examples illustrate how young children can be engaged in metacognition and self-regulation processes if provided with a structure for reflection and follow-up interactions with their teachers to help them consciously think about their learning and how they met their goals. In a further example of metacognitive activity, Angelica, a student in a fifth-grade classroom, decides that she needs some feedback from her teacher about a strategy she used to open her argument about how and why people need to be environmentally conscious:

A: I'm working on my draft. And I want to get your feedback.

T: Okay, so do we have our success criteria here, our checklist?

A: Yes.

T: What are you focusing on?

A: I'm working on this one, clarity.

T: So what do you think so far?

A: I don't know if I should . . . because I started with two questions and then I ended with a period and then I started with another question.

T: I see. So let's read it and see how that makes sense.

(Angelica reads her text aloud)

T: Okay, so let's go back to your original concern. So you're concerned about having two questions at the beginning. Well the question that you have here at the beginning, "I wonder why people don't pick the trash up?" Well you're following that up with what? What is this? "People may argue that . . ." What is that?

A: Umm that's a counterargument.

T: That's a counterargument. So this question, "I wonder why people don't pick up trash . . ."

A: Is connected to my counterargument.

T: Is connected to your counterargument. So it makes sense. Okay? So, what's the other question that you feel maybe . . .

A: I was going to put right here after, "About 33 million people don't care about the earth," I was going to put, "I wonder why they don't care?" and then I was going to put this one (Angelica points to the second question).

T: Oh, I see.

A: And I wanted to know if that was okay . . . to put two questions in a . . . a question period, then another question.

T: Well I think that, "I wonder why they don't care," and, "I wonder why people don't pick up trash," . . . it's connected, so is there a way that you think that maybe you can combine those two into one so that you don't have two questions back to back?

A: Yeah.

T: So can you think about that? Because, "I wonder why they don't care," and, "I wonder why people don't pick up trash" . . .

A: Are the same.

T: Are connected to each other. So you can definitely think about connecting those two so that it's one question but that has those two things, those two components that you wanted to make sure that were in there.

A: Okay.

T: So go ahead and think about how you can do that.

A: Yes, I will. Thanks.

In this example, we can see Angelica actively monitoring her writing composition. She wishes her argument to be clear to the reader and has raised questions in her own mind about whether the device she uses to begin her composition is effective. Not able to resolve these questions herself, she requests assistance from her teacher. She shows that she is conscious of her own learning and has made a decision that teacher feedback at this stage would help her resolve her question. She is well versed in the idea of feedback as a scaffold for learning as we discussed in the previous chapter. Rather than relying entirely on her teacher's direction, from her previous classroom experiences, Angelica has learned how to use her teacher as a resource in her learning, and this is well illustrated in their interaction. It seems clear that Angelica is well on the way to acquiring metacognitive skills and, in so doing, is developing the capacity of learning how to learn.

However, students like Angelica do not develop metacognitive skills automatically. Students need to be taught to use them effectively in support of their own learning. In the next section, we consider how teachers can assist students to acquire metacognitive skills in the context of formative assessment so that they develop some of the practices associated with learning how to learn.

LEARNING HOW TO LEARN: SUPPORTING METACOGNITION AND SELF-REGULATION

Cognitive and Evaluative Maps

The eminent psychologist Mary Alice White once observed that all too often students' experience of school resembles that of an adult sailing across an unknown sea, to an unknown destination.

> An adult would be desperate to know where he is going. But a child only knows he is going to school . . . The chart is neither available nor understandable to him. He does not even know how long the voyage will take. Very quickly, the daily life on board ship becomes all important . . . The daily chores, the demands, the inspections, become the reality, not the voyage, nor the destination.[14]

Although she made this observation from her research on students' views of the classroom over forty years ago, White's view remains an evocative analysis that still is true of students' experiences in many classrooms today. In such classrooms students are unclear about what it is they are supposed to be learning, or why, or how the lesson fits into a bigger picture of learning. They are unsure about whether, or how, what they are doing today connects to what they learned yesterday, last week, or last month. The lesson is solely under the direction of the teacher, and its central focus—for teacher and student alike—is on the completion of tasks. In essence, these classrooms privilege activities and products over the process of learning, its goals and trajectories. These circumstances leave students at a real distance, effectively disabling them from developing the practices of learning how to learn.

In contrast, in the process of formative assessment, as we saw in chapter 2, teachers, or teachers and students together have identified short-term learning goals that ideally represent a step on the path toward expertise in relation to an idea or skill in a subject matter area. The learning goal does not indicate what the students will do, or what activities or tasks they will engage in, but instead specifies what the next move in learning will be. As a step along the path toward increasing expertise, the learning goal should be connected to what came before and to what will come next, and thus provide the students with a cognitive map to the learning terrain. With connected learning goals, learning can become intentional—students know what they are learning and why, and teachers can assist them to achieve the goal.[15] When the learning goal is accompanied by clear success criteria—what the students will say, do, make, or write to indicate progress—students also have a clear "evaluative map," the frame of reference that the teacher and students will use to monitor their learning as it develops.[16] When students have both a clear cognitive map and a clear evaluative map, the authority in the classroom can be rebalanced from a situation where teachers are the "directors" of activity, to one in which students are able take on the role of a learner and, with teacher assistance, engage in metacognitive activity: self-monitoring and self-regulation.

Helping students understand the goal being aimed for and the indictors of progress is a first step in self-monitoring and self-regulation. The second is for students to monitor their learning and make judgments about their progress with respect to the criteria. Teachers can assist students to develop self-monitoring skills through models, tools, and providing opportunities to make decisions about action and feedback. These forms of assistance are discussed in turn below.

Models

Teachers provide models of metacognitive strategies that students can incorporate into their own repertoire. The way a teacher formulates questions provides models for students to ask themselves questions while they are learning. For example, questions designed to reveal evidence of thinking, one of the signature pedagogies for formative assessment, can be internalized by students and become a mechanism for self-monitoring. Questions such as "Why do you think that?"; "What is your evidence?"; and "How did you arrive at that conclusion?" probe students' reasoning and are questions students can ask themselves during learning. Questions designed to challenge thinking can be similarly appropriated by students, for example, "Does it always work that way?" or "How does this idea square with what was said earlier?"[17]

The questioning techniques that teachers employ to stimulate students' reflection about their learning also provide a resource that can be gradually internalized by students. For example, in mathematics questions such as "How does this problem connect to other types of problems you have solved?"; "Why did you choose that strategy to solve the problem?"; "Do you think your strategy was effective?"; "Are there alternate strategies you could try?"; and "Does this solution make sense?" can be incorporated by students into their self-monitoring repertoire. They can then be used to structure internal conversations while they engage in a task. Similarly, when students are involved in written composition, as our example above showed, they can be encouraged to externalize their cognitive procedures in a two-way interaction with their teacher.[18] In addition, in the context of writing, teachers can model a range of questions that can eventually be internalized by the students, for example: "How could you develop this idea?"; "How could you add interest to this point?"; and "What might be another good point to include on the other side of this argument?"

Tools

As we saw in the classroom examples, teachers can provide specific tools for student self-monitoring, ranging from graphic organizers, to exit tickets for reflections on success criteria, to reflection/planning logs. However, just giving such tools to students does not necessarily mean they will acquire the skills of self-monitoring. Assisting students to analyze the purposes and uses of the tools is a necessary precursor to students actively incorporating them in their own practice. Once students have used the tools to monitor and evaluate learning or to set goals, it is essential for teachers to spend time discussing the students' own comparative judgments with them. Only when teachers have had such discussions can they determine how well students' self-monitoring skills are developing, and provide any assistance they might need for further refinement. For instance, as in the case of the Ms. Pernisi's exit ticket example, the teacher can enhance students' evaluative skills by discussing with them the reasons for their personal ratings. And self-monitoring is similarly enhanced in the example from Ms. Wilson's class when she takes the time to discuss how well the student met her goal, and how she knows this. Furthermore, when teachers take the time to consider the results of the use of the tools on students' self-monitoring, with discussions about how the tool helped them make judgments about their learning and what else they might need, their experience of metacognition is deepened and enriched.

It should be noted that learning the skills of self-monitoring is an ongoing process and needs to be consistently included in students' classroom experience. By practicing the use of self-monitoring strategies and discussing them with their teachers, students will develop the capacity to prompt themselves and monitor their own learning without teacher support.

Opportunities to Engage in Self-Regulation

Recall that self-regulation involves goal setting, planning what to do next, evaluating and revising strategies, and determining when to seek assistance, all of which are important aspects in developing the capacities of learning how to learn. If students are going to become self-regulated learners, then they must have the opportunities and support to acquire the necessary skills. Returning to the classroom examples, we see instances of students engaged in self-regulation: setting goals or making plans based on the judgments they have made about learning.

Students' planning and goal setting are included in the structures and opportunities each of the teachers provides within their classroom experience. For example, in the first-grade class, the students set a goal at the end of each week, in the second-grade classroom the students plan their approach to reading each day, in the sixth-grade math class the students indicate what they think they need to work on next to increase their understanding, and in the social-studies high-school class the students make specific plans for how they will manage any difficulties that arise. In each case, the students meaningfully share responsibility with teachers for the assessment of their learning, and engage in decision-making about what they need next to advance.

Once again students should not be left to their own devices without any teacher intervention or monitoring. Rather, the teacher should discuss with the students their plans and use this time to help each student consider the appropriateness of the goal and plan. In a sense, this discussion time becomes another opportunity for metacognitive activity through which the students can consider whether the goal they have set in relation to their personal evaluations is the right one for them.

Establishing a community of practice for formative assessment through the signature pedagogies described in chapter 1 provides the context for students to engage in self-regulation. For example, when Angelica evaluates her own strategies while developing her argumentation writing and determines when to seek targeted assistance from her teacher, it is evident that the community of practice established in her classroom enables this opportunity. Angelica understands her role as an active agent in charge of her own learning, and is a partner in learning with her teacher. Similarly, the students in the other classroom examples have the expectations, routines, and support structures that enable their agency in learning so that they acquire competence in the skills of learning how to learn. Above all, however, these students will understand that the teachers value and respect them as capable learners who can increasingly take responsibility for the management of their learning in partnership with the teacher and with their peers.

Feedback

John Hattie and Helen Timperley suggested that teacher feedback can be focused at the self-regulation level. In the context of self-regulation, they proposed three questions as guides for students and for teachers:

1. Where am I going? (What are the goals?)
2. How am I going? (What progress is being made toward the goal?)
3. Where to next? (What activities need to be undertaken to make better progress?)[19]

To be self-regulated, students ultimately need to internalize these questions and actively use them in the process of learning. Teacher feedback that addresses these questions will provide students with models and strategies that they can incorporate into their own practices as learners.

The first question, "Where am I going?" is addressed when students have a clear conception of the learning goal and the success criteria as described above. The second question, "How am I going?" is answered when teachers provide feedback that is focused on the degree to which the students have attained the success criteria, the critical dimensions of the learning goal. In addition, students are provided with models of how to evaluate the evidence in relation to the criteria. The third question, "Where to next?" is answered when teacher feedback addresses what action the student can take to move forward. Hattie and Timperley noted that when feedback that "leads to greater possibilities for learning" is provided, it can have some of the most powerful effects on learning.[20] This idea is illustrated in a study conducted by Day and Cordón who found when students "get stuck" it is not necessary for teachers to give complete solutions.[21] Students learned better when they were given an indication of where they should look for a solution. This response encouraged them to adopt a "mindful" approach and active engagement, which is not the case when teachers correct students' work.[22]

Students need to build their own repertoire of self-regulation strategies. When they incorporate the hints, cues, or suggestions that teachers provide in their regulatory feedback to enhance learning, they learn specific strategies that they can draw on in future situations. We saw the kind of feedback that supports students' self-regulation in the earlier example of Angelica and her teacher. In their conversation, the teacher does not tell Angelica exactly what to do. Instead, she gives Angelica an idea that she can think about to improve her opening paragraph. The strategy of considering what the questions are really focused on, and connecting ideas related to the same topic in one question is not simply one that can sharpen her thinking on this occasion, it is also one Angelica can employ in the future.

It should be stressed that, with respect to feedback and self-regulation, if students are not given the opportunity to use the feedback, then there is little chance for them to develop the self-regulation skills the feedback is intended to support. In addition, if students do not use the feedback in relation to their work, the feedback will not have an impact on students' first-order skills, that is, what they are currently learning. In both instances, if the feedback is not used it merely becomes a time-wasting event for teachers and students. Teachers need to make time in the learning process for students to both incorporate the feedback and to consider the effects of the feedback on their subsequent improvements.

Metacognitive skills develop over time, with models and strategies provided by the teacher and practiced by the students with discussions about the strategies as they learn how to use them.[23] An important point to note here is that teaching metacognitive skills (including self-regulation) should be undertaken in the subject matter that students learn.[24] Metacognitive strategies are not generic across domains.[25] For example, strategies learned in the context of mathematical problem solving, science investigations, or written composition will not necessarily be transferable to other domains. In fact, efforts to treat them as such have largely resulted in failure.[26]

The ultimate goal is that students can monitor their learning and act on the internal feedback they generate without support. In short, they acquire the skills of learning how to learn.

MOTIVATION AND SELF-EFFICACY

Teachers who assist their students to develop metacognitive skills bring to their classrooms a growth mind-set (discussed in chapter 1). A growth mind-set refers to the belief that all children can learn and that everyone's intellectual capacity can grow.[27] Students also need to develop and apply a growth mind-set to their own learning. They must believe that they can learn and that their own intellectual capacity can grow. The idea of a growth mind-set is salient in the literature on motivation and self-efficacy, notably in Carol Dweck's work. Dweck proposed that there are two views of intelligence: an entity view and an incremental view.[28] People who have an entity view consider intelligence or ability as fixed and stable. Students with an entity view of intelligence are oriented to performance goals. They want to perform better than others, and they limit themselves to tasks they can succeed in so as to avoid failure. People who have an incremental view of intelligence believe intelligence or ability can be changed. Students with this view of intelligence are focused on learning and mastery as opposed to performance goals. They are interested in learning and meeting challenges and believe that effort, engagement in learning, and strategy development can lead to increased intelligence. By comparison with performance-oriented students, incrementalists are not preoccupied with failure, but instead value opportunities to revise learning strategies so as to be successful.

An important part of the "hidden curriculum" of formative assessment lies in its capacity to nurture the incrementalist view of ability, and thus to nourish motivations that favor lifelong learning. When teachers assist students in monitoring their learning and generating internal feedback, when they provide feedback to them at the level of self-regulation, and when they enable students to take action based on the sources of feedback available to them, they intrinsically support an incremental view of learning, and the student stance of proactive self-efficacy associated with it.

To this point, we have considered the development of metacognitive skills in connection with the support provided by teachers. In the next section, we will consider how peers can support metacognition.

PEER-ASSESSMENT AND FEEDBACK

Another approach to supporting students in the development of metacognitive skills is providing opportunities for peer-assessment and feedback. Peer-assessment and feedback involves students in evaluating others' progress in relation to the success criteria and providing suggestions about improvements. To illustrate, let us consider these exchanges between two pairs of high school students in a geography class. Prior to the students' beginning their own work, as a class, they had evaluated other students' essays on a different topic that focused on the same criteria. After a period of independent writing the students provide feedback to each other on what they have written so far. The topic is the geographic significance of freeways.

Pair One:

S1: So you need to do more on the causes that affect the consequences, list more causes, and give more locational details.

S2: Okay. Umm, you did everything good. You gave lots of locational detail, you named the freeways, and all of your ideas were developed. And your only thing is to give a post factor because you gave a before factor and you gave a consequence as well, which is good.

Pair Two:

S1: Well because that's one of things I felt you did well. You put a lot of causes, even though you didn't do the consequences, you've done a lot of causes. But I think you need to develop them a bit more saying why it's happening and where it's happening.

S2: For the causes?

S1: Yeah, for the causes. But you need to do the consequences as well.

S2: Okay. Thanks.

These students clearly understand the criteria that their work is expected to meet. Because they are clear about what the criteria entail, they are able to compare their peers' current work with the criteria and make a judgment about the degree to which the criteria have been met. Then, based on this comparison, they make suggestions to their peers for improvement. They have transferred the internal process they use in regulating their learning to their peers' learning. It may be that first learning these skills in the context of someone else's learning can help students develop the skills to make judgments about evidence in relation to specific goals, which can then be transferred when students engage in and regulate their own learning.[29]

As is the case for self-monitoring and self-regulation, peer-assessment and feedback skills are not acquired automatically but need to be taught. As we see in the example above, understanding what meeting the success criteria involves is an essential first step. The models teachers provide through their feedback practices will be a valuable learning opportunity for students to develop their own feedback skills. In addition, teachers can assist students by providing prompts for them to use in either class discussion where they provide feedback on each other's ideas, or in one-on-one peer contexts. For example, in a third-grade classroom the teacher uses these prompts (see figure 5.5) to help students give feedback to each other. They are posted in the classroom as reminders.

FIGURE 5.5
Classroom Poster of Conversation Prompts

CONVERSATION PROMPTS

- I'd like to suggest . . .
- Have you thought about . . .
- I didn't understand what you meant when you said . . .
- A strength I see in your work is . . .
- I notice that . . . I agree with . . . I disagree with . . .
- You could improve this by . . .

In a classroom with younger students—first graders—the teacher works with the students to develop behaviors that support positive interactions, a prerequisite for peer feedback. She also posts a chart in the classroom (see figure 5.6) and spends time modeling with students what these behaviors look like.

This teacher also models effective feedback to her students by using sticky notes to provide feedback on students' math-problem-solving strategies that are displayed on bulletin boards around the classroom. The students add to the teacher's feedback on their peers' work. Students are also encouraged to respond to the feedback they have received from both teacher and peers, and so a dialogue is begun.

When students engage in the assessment of their peers, they gain a wider view of what is possible. Their exploration of others' learning allows them to see different ways of approaching tasks, and, as a result, extend their own repertoire of strategies, so contributing to self-regulation capacities. In addition, it is possible for students to become clearer about their own learning by providing feedback about someone else's. This may result in the learning of new, more effective strategies.[30]

Assisting students to effectively provide feedback to each other is not a one-time occurrence. Instead, teachers engage in helping students build skills over time, involving them in the process of monitoring how well they are developing. This involvement can include class discussions about how peer-assessment is working, what counts as appropriate and inappropriate feedback, and what the students need to do to enhance their skills, as well as providing individual assistance to students,

FIGURE 5.6
Classroom Poster of Behaviors for Working with a Partner

WORKING WITH A PARTNER	
LOOKS LIKE . . .	**SOUNDS LIKE . . .**
* Turn toward partner	* Compliments
* Maintaining eye contact when talking	* 6 inch voice
* Stay on task	* Asking questions
* Sitting close	* Pleasant voice

and giving feedback to the students about the quality of their peer feedback and suggestions for improvement. This process of continual monitoring, feedback, and assistance is an important component to making peer feedback a routine practice in the classroom.

It is evident that to engage in the forms of peer feedback just described requires a classroom community in which students feel safe to share their thinking, to give and to receive feedback, and to learn with and from each other. As discussed in chapter 1, establishing such a classroom community must be one of the core goals for teachers in the practice of formative assessment.

TEACHER KNOWLEDGE AND SKILLS

Before considering the knowledge and skills teachers need to support students' metacognition, it is important to note that without a growth mind-set—a belief that all students can learn, that each one has the capacity to become a competent and capable learner, and that all the students must, in the end, learn for themselves—the opportunities for developing metacognitive skills are likely to be absent from the classroom. When teachers adopt these perspectives, then they are more likely to recognize that their role is to support students to acquire the skills of learning how to learn.

As we have seen in this chapter, metacognition is a hallmark of effective learning. It will be necessary for teachers to know what metacognition, including self-regulation, entails, and how these ideas relate to becoming a competent learner. In other words, they need to know how metacognition is a significant dimension of learning how to learn. Experience suggests that these ideas are woefully under-represented in both preservice and in-service education. Furthermore, in recent reform initiatives, for example, the focus on standards to enable students to become college and career ready, there is little or no attention paid to these vital learning skills. Understanding how the practice of formative assessment can support meta-cognition can be a productive avenue for teachers to develop this knowledge.

This chapter described various means through which teachers can support students to develop metacognitive skills. These, and other methods teachers devise, will provide the accumulated resources that they can deploy in their pedagogy to support students' self-monitoring and self-regulation. In addition to assembling such resources, teachers will need planning and management skills to include opportunities in the classroom for students to engage in metacognitive activity. For example, as Ms. Pernisi noted in her quote earlier in the chapter, she now "does less"—not so many activities—so as to include time in the lesson for student reflection. All the teachers in the classroom examples at the beginning of the chapter organized and managed their classrooms so that they had time to focus on conversations with their students about their self-assessment, goal setting, or planning. Similarly, if students are to engage in peer-assessment and feedback, then teachers need the organizational and management skills for this to occur on a regular basis in their classrooms.

Teachers also need to know that it takes consistent practice over time for students to develop self-monitoring and self-regulation skills. Teaching metacognitive skills is not something that is undertaken sporadically or infrequently. Rather, through the practice of formative assessment and the implementation of the signature pedagogies discussed in chapter 1, developing metacognition becomes part of the fabric of learning in the classroom.

Students' metacognitive activity is neither an optional extra, nor a luxury.[31] Unless they are able to evaluate their own strengths and needs and how they might deal with them, students will be less likely to become successful. Moreover, the core goals of a student's rights approach to assessment—students' best interests as a primary concern, student engagement in all decisions affecting them, and no students adversely impacted by assessment practices—as well as those of personalized learning will likely not receive the attention that they warrant.

Finally, metacognitive skills and motivations are essential elements in the formation of the lifelong learning abilities that Seymour Papert argued are the true competitive skills of the twenty-first century. Because no one else can learn for them, students have to be active agents in their own learning. The future of our society, and of the individuals within it, depends in no small measure on our commitment to developing these skills in our students. In the context of ever-changing demands on learners across the life course, the opportunity to develop these skills is the ultimate children's right. Upholding this right is something for which each one of us is responsible. Is this not our real obligation in terms of "high-stakes" accountability?

In the book's final chapter, we turn to a consideration of policies that can support widespread implementation of formative assessment practices.

CHAPTER 6

Policy Support for
Formative Assessment*

As we have seen in this book, formative assessment is a set of practices enacted by teachers and their students that has been shown to improve learning. In the United States, formative assessment is a reemerging idea. This reemergence is encapsulated by noted measurement expert, Lorrie Shepard, in her 2005 observation that "Recently, this robust and well-researched knowledge base has made its way back across the oceans, offering great promise for shifting classroom practices toward a culture of learning."[1]

In the United States, interest in reforming assessment practices emerged during the 1980s and 1990s. This interest was motivated by the increased use of standardized tests, mounting evidence that these tests were narrowing the curriculum being taught (in part due to the extensiveness of many standards that pushed curricula towards being "a mile wide and an inch deep"[2]), and research in cognitive and motivational psychology that pointed the way for new forms of assessment.[3] However, the reemergence of formative assessment in the United States at the beginning of the twenty-first century coincided with an era of test-based high-stakes accountability. Initially implemented by states, test-based accountability has been accelerated in the United States through federal legislation. The No Child

*This chapter was co-authored with E. Caroline Wylie, senior research scientist in the Cognitive and Learning Sciences Center at Educational Testing Service. Any opinions expressed in this chapter are those of the author and not necessarily of Educational Testing Service.

Left Behind Act (NCLB) enacted in 2002 imposed a single test-based account-ability model on each state, requiring annual testing of students against state standards in reading and mathematics in grades 3–8, with sanctions for schools failing to meet achievement targets. While some have argued that the advent of accountability systems has led to improvements in student achievement, others regard the improvements as modest and suggest that these improvements do not fulfill the aspirations that accountability systems were established to attain.[4] In addition, it appears that test-based accountability systems have led to an increased emphasis on "tested" subjects at the expense of those not included in the account-ability program, teaching to the test, and focusing on what are sometimes termed "bubble" students—those who are close to attaining proficiency—at the expense of those who are further away from proficiency. In more extreme cases there has also been evidence of excluding low performing students from the tests, providing help to students while the assessments were administered, and changing student responses after they have finished.[5]

However one views these accountability systems, an outcome is the creation of "multiple assessment systems, all geared to serving the summative function of assessment, so marginalizing, and denying time to, assessment that supports learn-ing."[6] Given the pressures on the assessment system, such as sanctions associated with failure to make adequate yearly progress, Shepard's hopes for shifting class-room practice to a *culture of learning* have been impeded by the prevalence of a *culture of testing* that now predominates in schools, districts, and states. The latter is underscored by the increase in expenditure by states and districts on summa-tive and interim assessments. In 1997, annual sales were estimated at $260 million, while by 2009 they had almost tripled to $700 million, a figure that likely underes-timates expenditure because it does not include assessment preparation materials.[7] It is not that the expenditures themselves are problematic per se, rather it is the implicit message of the relative importance conveyed by the imbalance in expendi-tures between formative and summative assessment. It is too early to tell what the impact will be of the Common Core State Standards (CCSS) and the associated next-generation assessments, to be discussed later in this chapter.

Despite the growing global awareness of the benefits of formative assessment, the adoption of formative assessment practices in many countries, and the efforts of individual states in the United States to support formative assessment practices through statewide professional development (e.g., North Carolina, Iowa, and Michigan), there is little in current U.S. national policy agendas to restrain the culture of testing and to support widespread formative assessment implementation.[8]

The aim of this chapter is to consider the policy agendas and practical support emanating from policy that are needed in the United States to transform a culture of testing into a culture of learning. We begin with a consideration of policy foundations from a number of countries and systems that promote formative assessment as an integral component of high-quality and high-equity outcomes. This is followed by a discussion of how national and regional policies can support the involvement of students in the assessment process, which is a key element of the children's rights perspective taken throughout this book. Then we consider the relationship between formative and summative assessment from the policy perspective of a number of countries. Next is a discussion of the role of external assessment and a subsequent review of the role of teacher judgment in several countries' assessment systems. The chapter concludes with a consideration of how formative assessment could be better supported in the U.S. policy context.

POLICY FOUNDATIONS FOR FORMATIVE ASSESSMENT

Between 2002 and 2004, the Organisation for Economic Co-operation and Development (OECD) examined policy and practices with respect to formative assessment in eight education systems (Denmark; England; Italy; Labrador, Canada; New Zealand; Newfoundland, Canada; Queensland, Australia; and Scotland).[9] The most recent comprehensive summary of OECD member countries' practices in formative assessment is the influential 2006 OECD report on higher education. This report makes clear that the national and regional governments of each of the eight systems supported formative assessment practice, motivated by evidence of the impact on student learning, as a means to broader policy ends. Formative assessment was promoted to better enable teachers to meet the needs of increasingly diverse student populations, to close gaps in the equity of student outcomes, and meet the goals of lifelong learning.[10] Each one of these policy goals is consistent with the students' rights approach to assessment that has been interwoven through-out this book in our consideration of formative assessment practice.

Although there was not a common definition across the OCED systems for for-mative assessment, there were key elements that echo themes in the earlier chapters and that teachers incorporated into practice.

- Establishment of a classroom culture that encourages interaction and the use of assessment tools;
- Establishment of learning goals and tracking of individual student progress toward those goals;
- Use of varied instruction methods to meet diverse students needs;
- Use of varied approaches to assessing student understanding;
- Feedback on student performance and adaptation of instruction to meet iden-tified needs; and
- Active involvement of students in the learning process.[11]

Across the eight systems a range of policy frameworks was established, along with resources and incentive structures to support teachers' formative assessment in their classrooms. Examples of the policies and resources to support formative assessment are:

- *Denmark and Italy:* Legislation promoting and supporting the practice of for-mative assessment and establishing it as a priority.
- *England; New Zealand; Queensland, Australia; and Scotland:* Guidelines on effective teaching and formative assessment embedded in national curriculum and other materials.
- *Newfoundland and Labrador, Canada; and New Zealand:* Provision of tools and exemplars to support effective formative assessment.
- *Italy and New Zealand:* Investments in initiatives and special programs incor-porating formative approaches.
- *New Zealand and Queensland, Australia:* Investment in teacher professional development on formative assessment from the government level.[12]

Since the OECD study, England has made considerable investments in support-ing teachers to implement formative assessment effectively and to tackle inconsistencies in practice throughout the country. In 2008, Jim Knight, U.K. Minister of State for Schools and Learners, announced that

> Many schools are already seeing the benefits of using assessment for learning practices and resources, but I want all schools to have access to high-quality training and support so that assessment for learning can be embedded in all classrooms. That is why the Government has invested £150 million over the next three years for continuing professional development for teachers in assessment for learning.[13]

Scotland also has a history of promoting formative assessment. In a range of policy documents dating from 1991, assessment that occurs on a day-to-day basis has been regarded as an important and integral part of the learning and teaching process.[14] More recently, policy documents have included a commitment to involve all schools in formative assessment, or as it is called in Scotland, Assessment Is For Learning (AifL).[15] The commitment to AifL has been backed by the provision of extensive online professional-development materials, including exemplars of practice in varying local circumstances.[16]

Outside the member countries of the OECD, policy documents in Hong Kong make a number of recommendations for the development of assessment for learning, including the following: "a) Develop more diversified modes of assessment and a reduction in tests and examinations; b) Use assessments that probe higher-order thinking skills, creativity and understanding rather than rote memorization of facts."[17] However, as David Carless from the University of Hong Kong reported, the main challenges for formative assessment in Hong Kong "are overcoming the deeply entrenched view of assessment as summative and competitive; the associated focus on performance rather than mastery; and teachers' limited understandings of and sympathies for formative assessment."[18]

From this discussion of policies and resources put in place to support formative assessment, we can conclude that many national and regional governments regard formative assessment as a means to achieve the policy goal of improved educational outcomes for all children and have committed resources to support its implementation. It is noteworthy that the resources policymakers have committed are primarily focused on providing professional development for teachers so that they can "use the elements of formative assessment as an overall approach to teaching and learning, changing the culture of their classrooms."[19] In this context, it is instructive to consider the policy context in the United States for improved learning.

U.S. Policy Context

Over the past several decades in the United States, test-based accountability has been a centerpiece of reform agendas designed to improve education. The prevailing theory of action underlying these reform agendas is that by establishing standards, assessing the achievement of students annually against the standards, and holding teachers and schools accountable for student achievement through a range of sanctions if targets are not met, there will be a concomitant improvement in teaching and learning. The policy objectives of NCLB were to: 1) increase student achievement so that all students attain proficiency, or better, in reading and mathematics by 2014; and 2) reduce the achievement gap for traditionally underserved populations.

As noted earlier, NCLB has not led to the hoped-for improvements in education.[20] Consequently, spurred by the relative performance of U.S. students to those in OECD systems among others, and the potential associated detriments to the U.S. economy and to individual citizens, the Common Core State Standards have been adopted by 46 states and the District of Columbia. The Common Core State Standards define grade level expectations required for students to be college and career ready at the end of grade 12. In addition, two federally funded and state-led assessment consortia are developing "next-generation" assessments that will be used to gauge the achievement of students relative to standards on an annual basis. The estimated $350 million that is being expended by the federal government for state consortia to develop next-generation assessments is further testament to the culture of testing that prevails in the United States. While each assessment consortia has spent some money on formative assessment and support materials, there is an imbalance between the investment in summative assessment and the investment in formative assessment. This is not to say that we should invest less in the summative, only to note that there should be a better balance between the two expenditures.

It is clear that a least two of the elements comprising the earlier reform theory of action are still in place: standards and annual assessment of all students in grades 3–8 and high school.[21] In terms of assessment, it is also clear that policymakers are more focused on summative testing, rather than formative assessment, as the primary mechanism for improvement. To draw a further contrast between the perspectives of some of the other OECD systems and that of the United States, it is instructive to look at how formative assessment is treated in the context of next-generation assessment systems in the United States. Formative assessment is generally included as a component of the assessment system along with summative and interim/benchmark measures and is considered one of the instruments available to teachers to improve teaching and learning.[22] For example, a policy brief on comprehensive assessment systems from the Alliance for Excellent Education suggests that "such a system would include formative assessments that show teachers whether students truly understand the content or where they are struggling, along with tools to suggest steps they could take to help students overcome their difficulties."[23] The use of formative assessment proposed here suggests more of a remediation response to assessment, rather than contingent learning. Contingent learning occurs when teachers and students take the opportunity to build on what students already know to move them incrementally from their current state of learning to a more advanced state. It is important that all students' learning is contingent (see discussions on contingent planning and learning in chapter 4). Contingent learning is central to the practice of formative assessment and to a children's rights perspective on assessment. Conceptualizations of formative assessment as an instrument perpetuate a focus on the formative/summative distinction couched as alternative methods of evaluating learning. Lost in this comparison are the distinctive roles and practices of both teachers and students in formative assessment per se that render it such a powerful engine for teaching and learning.[24]

As noted earlier, one of the policy objectives of OECD systems that support formative assessment is lifelong learning. Despite calls in the United States for all students to be college and career ready by grade 12, the emphasis on college and career readiness through the CCSS is primarily on learning content and the skills and practices associated with subject matter. Although the CCSS have a strong emphasis on mathematical practices and on literacy across the content areas, the important skill of learning how to learn (see chapter 5) is still largely absent from discussions about college and career readiness. The next section describes policies that have been adopted by countries that promote an active role for students in the assessment process so as the assist them in developing lifelong learning skills.

STUDENT ROLE IN ASSESSMENT

The OECD reports that "all the national and regional governments participating in the OECD study promote formative assessment as a means to meeting the goals of lifelong learning."[25] Recall from chapter 5 that students' involvement in the process of formative assessment can support them to become active, autonomous learners who can take responsibility for their own learning. These are the outcomes of formative assessment that support the goals of lifelong learning.

In Canadian policy documents, student involvement in formative assessment is referred to as "assessment *as* learning." Policy guidelines make clear that "assessment *as* learning" is an integral component of formative assessment policy. For example, the Western and Northern Canadian Protocol provides the following guidelines:

> Assessment *as* learning focuses on the explicit fostering of students' capacity over time to be their own best assessors, but teachers need to start by presenting and modeling external, structured opportunities for students to assess themselves.[26]

Similarly, the Ontario Ministry of Education promotes the student role in assessment:

> Teachers engage in assessment *as* learning by helping all students develop their capacity to be independent, autonomous learners who are able to set individual goals, monitor their own progress, determine next steps, and reflect on their thinking and learning.[27]

Scottish government assessment policy makes clear that "learners at all stages should be involved in planning and reflecting on their own learning, through formative approaches, self- and peer assessment and personal learning planning."[28] A similar perspective is echoed in Hong Kong policy documents with calls to provide opportunities to do assessment collaboratively with students, to encourage them to carry out peer or self-assessment, and to share with students the goals of learning, so that they can recognize the standards they are aiming for.[29]

Scandinavian policies also make provision for a student role in assessment. For example, Denmark and Finland place primary emphasis on student self-evaluation. Finnish policy regards a focus on student self-assessment as more important than comparisons among students.[30] Legislation in Norway makes provision for self-assessment with regulations establishing that each student "shall participate actively in the assessment of his or her own work, own competence and own academic development."[31] In Sweden, formative assessment is supported by Individual Development Plans (IDPs). The process of developing IDPs focuses on engaging students in setting goals for learning and developing skills for self- and peer-assessment.[32]

As in the Scandinavian countries, in New Zealand, formative assessment is at the heart of the country's assessment strategy. New Zealand's assessment strategy emphasizes the development of the students' own capacity to regulate their own learning through self-assessment. Assessment policy in New Zealand has focused on improving student learning by building students' assessment ability through active involvement in assessment.[33]

Against this background of the inclusion of students in formative assessment, it is striking to note that policy documents in the United States are largely silent on this topic. In considerations about next-generation assessments, the role of the student is absent. This may well be because of the prevailing view of formative assessment as an instrument. Within this conception, students have no role other than to receive pronouncements of their learning status. It is regrettable that an important opportunity to emphasize the role of the student in assessment and the desirable outcomes of that role in terms of lifelong learning are being missed in current U.S. policy initiatives.

We noted earlier that U.S. policymakers continue to operate from the perspective that summative testing drives improvement. In the next sections we examine how formative and summative assessment are viewed from the policy perspective in other countries. We also consider the related and intertwined issues of external assessments and the role of teacher judgment.

THE RELATIONSHIP BETWEEN FORMATIVE AND SUMMATIVE ASSESSMENT

Reform efforts in Scotland have undergone several phases resulting in well-rounded policies and practical supports for teachers. A recent government document provides clear direction for both the central purpose of assessment and how that purpose may be achieved: "The central purpose of assessment is to support learning and this is best achieved by a combination of formative and summative assessment."[34] This point is echoed in comments by Janet Looney who observed in an OCED report on the integration of formative and summative assessment that "Scotland's own Assessment is for Learning (AifL) programme similarly encourages teachers to consider assessment as an integrated part of the teaching and learning process."[35]

In New Zealand there is an assumption, beginning at the level of the Ministry of Education, that teachers will be able to reliably make both formative and summative assessment judgments. There is also the assumption that multiple sources of evidence will be used to form a robust overall judgment. For example, the mathematics standards for years 1–8 notes:

> Multiple sources of evidence should inform overall teacher judgments about a student's performance. As well as the student's work, sources of evidence may include self- and peer-assessments, interviews, observations, and results from assessment tools. A single assessment is insufficient and unacceptable.[36]

In Norway teachers have primary responsibility for both formative and summative student assessment.[37] Although the role of summative grades is not emphasized until the upper levels of secondary schools for students' leaving certificates (the equivalent of high school diplomas), there is still an expectation of constant communication among teachers, students, and parents at all grades with monthly meetings to provide a forum for this information sharing. Similar to the Norwegian system, in Sweden the emphasis in the early grades is on formative assessment rather than summative. Teachers use a variety of evidence sources to inform their understanding of student progress and provide regular feedback to students.[38]

Nusche and colleagues described the Swedish approach to assessment as "a balanced approach" closely paralleling the use of the term "balanced assessment system" used by many U.S. states, for example, North Carolina and Virginia.[39] However, in contrast to the United States, where a "balanced system" tends to be construed as one in which additional assessment types such as interim or formative are added to the summative system, the Scandinavian approaches consider balanced to mean a de-emphasis on grades and summative assessment until the point that consequential—and less qualitative—judgments are really needed.

Closely related to role of summative assessments in general is the issue of the role of external assessments, standardized assessments that may be produced at either a state or national level. In what follows we consider the role of external assessments in a number of countries.

THE ROLE OF EXTERNAL ASSESSMENTS

In Australia each state and territory has its own external accreditation process, which both certifies school completion at year 12 and ranks students for entry into tertiary institutions. These external assessments have obvious high stakes for students. Up to year 12 there is no standard examination requirement to progress through elementary school or to gain acceptance into secondary school. However, the states and territories recognize that there is a role for monitoring student performance over time in key subject areas. For this purpose, a periodic sample testing approach called the National Assessment Program (NAP) is used. NAP is similar to the National Assessment of Educational Progress (NAEP) in the United States, which uses carefully constructed sampling frames to test samples of students approximately every two years in reading and mathematics at fourth, eighth, and twelfth grades, along with other subject areas on a less frequent basis.[40]

The purpose of NAP in Australia is to provide information so that "governments, education authorities and schools can determine whether or not young Australians are meeting important educational outcomes."[41] In addition to regular assessments of literacy and numeracy for all students in years 3, 5, 7, and 9, the NAP employs sample assessments that focus on science literacy (year 6), civics and citizenship (years 6 and 10), and information and communication technology (ICT) literacy (years 6 and 10). The sampling approach allows interested parties to have access to information that is sufficiently reliable to provide insights into progress on important outcomes, without overburdening students with external assessments that have little direct bearing on their education.

Other countries that do not emphasize summative tests for students until their later years in school use periodic external assessments to identify students' basic skills that require additional support. For example, in Norway students take mapping tests (years 1, 2, and 3) and national tests (years 4, 8, and 9).[42] In Sweden there is a system of national assessment at key stages (critical grade levels). Teachers mark the assessments for each of these stages. The assessments administered in years 3 and 5 are intended for diagnostic and formative purposes only, but teachers must take the results of year 9 assessments into consideration when setting final grades.[43]

In France a distinction is made between information that focuses on student learning and broader information that addresses school performance. Commenting on this distinction Paul Black and Dylan Wiliam noted

> The results achieved by students on external high-stakes tests are not seen as a good way of monitoring standards of achievement in schools . . . Instead, the Ministry of Education . . . monitors all aspects of educational provision, including facilities and resources, classroom practices, students' achievements and school effectiveness, through focused surveys.[44]

These surveys focus on both achievement as well as several noncognitive traits, such as attitudes and values. A sampling approach is used for these survey measures to provide information about students as they leave *collèges* at age 15.

In addition to the surveys that use sampling approaches to monitor student achievement, the French Ministry of Education also uses national external assessments to provide teachers with data on all of their individual students so as to guide instruction.

> A system was introduced of testing all students in alternate years at the ages of 8 and 11, and every year in all subjects for students at age 16. The formative purpose of these assessments was emphasized by having the tests set at the beginning of the school year, so that they inform each teacher about their new class.[45]

Given that these assessments are timed to take place early in the school year, they focus attention on the resulting information as "an aid to teaching, rather than a judgment of teachers."[46]

In the use of summative assessment across the countries discussed above, various approaches have been taken to maximize the benefits of external summative assessments while minimizing the potential negative effects. These include reducing the number of grade levels in which students are tested, using sampling approaches so that not all students are tested each year, and changing the timing of the assessment so that the results can only meaningfully be used to inform formative decisions.

The examples of external summative assessment stand in contrast to the U.S. perspective. In an era of high-stakes testing, all students, beginning in grade 3 are tested each year, resulting in U.S. students being some of the most tested children in the world.[47] Given that this testing regimen has not led to the hoped-for improvements in U.S. education, from a children's rights perspective, the question about assessment serving the best interests of students deserves to be raised.

Another point of contrast between the United States and several other OECD countries is in the role of teacher judgment in summative assessment. It is to teacher judgment that we now turn.

ROLE OF TEACHER JUDGMENT

In several countries, teacher judgment plays a significant role in summative or consequential decisions. In these instances, teacher judgment is generally employed through a process of moderation. Moderation refers to a set of approaches that can be taken to support the consistency of judgments among teachers and schools. For example, statistical moderation is a process that aims to adjust scores that were given by teachers deemed to be too lenient or severe. Another form of moderation, social or consensus moderation focuses on the calibration of teacher judgments through a structured exchange of student papers and discussion of scores.

New Zealand and Queensland, Australia, are two places where teacher moderation has been successfully used for many years. In New Zealand, teacher moderation within and between schools is a regular part of the assessment process. Part of a principal's task is to ensure that appropriate moderation processes are in place, in particular the moderation approaches that require teachers to share papers, and with the use of rubrics identify and agree on strengths and weaknesses shown in the student work.

While the introduction of teacher moderation raised concerns in terms of teacher workloads, the Ministry of Education recognizes the benefits it provides.[48] Teacher moderation:

- Brings together collective wisdom, resulting in greater consistency of judgment, and focused teaching;
- Provides greater confidence in teacher judgments, and assurance that judgments are consistent with those of other professionals;
- Leads to shared expectations of learning, and understandings of standards and progressions of learning;

- Develops deeper understandings about content and progressions of learning;
- Improves quality of assessment;
- Aligns expectations and judgments with standards or progressions, and hence improves teaching and learning; and
- Assures parents and others that interpretations of students' achievements are in line with those of other professionals.

From the perspective of over forty years of teacher moderation in Queensland, Australia, Valentina Klenowski and Claire Wyatt-Smith reinforced many of the benefits listed above in their thoughtful paper on standards, teacher judgment, and moderation. They noted that teacher moderation is a form of quality assurance on teacher judgment, supports a common understanding of standards and what represents achievement of those standards, benefits curriculum design and delivery, and builds teachers' assessment capacity and confidence in their assessment skills.[49] In Australia and New Zealand, teachers have an extensive history of honing their judgment skills in the context of summative assessment, skills that serve them well in the context of day-to-day judgments of formative assessment.

In the past, in England, high-stakes examinations consisted of a series of written papers, scored by external examiners (with a strong moderation process in place to support comparability of judgments). With the advent of the National Curriculum at the end of the 1980s came end-of-key-stage testing: key stage 1 for students aged 7, key stage 2 for students aged 11, and key stage 3 for students aged 14 in English, mathematics, and science (age 11 and 14 only), with teacher judgments of student performance reported in all other subjects at these ages. However, little guidance was provided about record keeping. As a result, teachers developed their own comprehensive record-keeping systems in an effort to show that teacher judgment could be done in a highly reliable and thorough way. However, these record-keeping systems, although detailed, did not adequately support the formative aspects of teaching and learning. As a consequence, the inclusion of teacher moderation contributed, in part, to a shift away from formative assessment in England.[50] This shift away from formative assessment has since been recognized by policymakers who have, as discussed earlier, committed extensive resources to professional support for teachers in this area.

HOW COULD U.S. POLICY BETTER SUPPORT FORMATIVE ASSESSMENT?

In contrast to many of the countries we have focused on in this chapter, the predominant paradigm for formative assessment in the United States persists as one of measurement. In this paradigm—created within a culture of testing—formative assessment is predominantly construed as a test.[51] This is not to say that an instrument cannot be used in the context of formative assessment. The information yielded from an instrument can provide indications of students' learning status relative to the "gap" so that teachers and students can use to make adjustments to learning as it develops. The point here is the relative emphasis given to formative assessment as an instrument. Notwithstanding references in one of the next-generation assessment proposals to formative assessment "tools and resources,"[52] the conception of formative assessment generally expressed is one of an instrument. This is a mistake. Absent from this view are notions of consistently working from students' emerging understandings within the Zone of Proximal Development,[53] supporting learning through instructional scaffolding, including feedback, and the active involvement of students in the assessment/learning process.

This mistaken conceptualization may cascade into the loss of important policy initiatives. The Race to the Top Assessment Program offers an unprecedented opportunity to initiate major changes in teaching and learning practices in the United States.[54] However, the vast sums of money available through this program are overwhelmingly channeled toward the development of summative assessments. We need summative assessments to support valid and reliable judgments about how learners are performing relative to the CCSS. This information can be fed back into the system to make programmatic and curricular decisions, among others. It is evident that the use of other summative assessments, often termed interim or benchmark assessments, is gaining ground in terms of their perceived, though empirically undocumented, significance for increasing achievement.[55] In the context of the current reform agendas, it would seem sensible for policies to be introduced that support a set of assessment practices that have been shown to make a difference in student achievement. As the 2006 OECD report noted "Teachers use the elements of formative assessment as an overall approach to teaching and learning, changing the culture of their classrooms. They point to improvements in the quality of teaching and learning, as well as in relationships with students and parents."[56] Surely these are goals that policymakers in the United States would want to support? So what can we do to support these goals?

Assessment Systems

In chapter 2, the idea of comprehensive, coherent, and continuous assessment systems was introduced. A system that embodies these characteristics would provide decision makers at all levels of the education system with the information they need to support student learning in both policy and practice. The 2006 OECD report on higher education urges countries to better align macro- and micro-level assessment policy approaches. At the most basic level, alignment means that education stakeholders ensure that policies do not compete with each other. We have seen in our earlier discussions how policy in several countries enables summative and formative assessment to cohabit without negatively impacting each other.

The OECD report goes on to suggest that better aligned macro- and micro-level policy approaches should enable the elements of formative and summative assessment to reinforce each other. If this were to occur, then the message to teachers would not be that summative assessment is the currency of the realm, but that formative assessment is also a significant part of the treasury. The role of teacher judgment would be recognized as an important component of day-to-day assessment practice.

Investing in Teachers

The 2006 OECD report also called on countries to strengthen the mix of policies and to make deeper investments to promote real changes in teaching and assessment throughout education systems. The report argued that a greater range of strategies in the policy mix will help support more consistent messages on the importance of formative assessment, more strategic investment of resources, and a change in culture at all levels of the education system.

Thus far, U.S. policy to improve education has centered on standards and summative assessment, with investments in tools not teachers. Rethinking policy to favor formative assessment as an integral part of educational reform as other OEDC countries have done, with a corresponding commitment of resources to provide teachers with the support they need to implement formative assessment effectively, would go a long way toward making formative assessment a reality across the

United States. Implementation of formative assessment practices in U.S. classrooms will necessitate sustained effort, and will require many teachers to make significant changes. We know that teacher change can be supported over time with systematic and consistent professional development.[57] Some states have already begun along this path and it is to be hoped that others will follow. If we believe the decades of research and theory that underpin the practice of formative assessment, we need to begin this journey—a journey with the destination of a *learning culture* rather than the *testing culture* that currently prevails.

To conclude this book, we return to where we began—the rights of children in assessment that came from the United Nations Convention on the Rights of the Child.[58] Recall the following exhortation: "those with responsibility for assessment will need to ensure that: the best interests of the child are a primary consideration in decision-making; that children are offered opportunities to participate meaningfully through the decision-making process; and that opportunities to learn, progress and succeed will be offered to children equally."[59] Policymakers will need to heed these words if they are intent on serving the best interests of children. One of the foremost ways they can pay heed is to ensure that their policies with respect to assessment enable the learning of all students, irrespective of context or circumstances. As we have seen in this book, formative assessment enables the learning of all students, and gives them the opportunity to learn, progress, and succeed equally.

Notes

Introduction

1. Margaret Heritage, "Gathering Evidence of Student Understanding," in *SAGE Handbook of Research on Classroom Assessment,* ed. James H. McMillan (Thousand Oaks, CA: SAGE Publications, 2012), 179–195.
2. Frederick Erickson, personal communication to author, October 28, 2009.
3. Terence J. Crooks, "The Impact of Classroom Evaluation Practices on Students," *Review of Educational Research* 58, no. 4 (1988): 438–81; Gary Natriello, "The Impact of Evaluation Processes on Students," *Educational Psychologist* 22, no. 2 (1987): 155–75; Paul J. Black and Dylan Wiliam, "Assessment and Classroom Learning," *Assessment in Education: Principles Policy and Practice* 5, no. 1 (1998): 7–73.
4. United Nations Convention on the Rights of the Child (UNCRC), "The UN Convention on the Rights of the Child," Centre for Studies on Inclusive Education, last modified July 20, 2010, http://www.csie.org.uk/inclusion/child-rights.shtml.
5. Jane Fortin, *Children's Rights and the Developing Law.* 2nd ed. (London, UK: Butterworths, 2003).
6. Jannette Elwood and Laura Lundy, "Revisioning Assessment Through a Children's Rights Approach: Implications for Policy, Process and Practice," *Research Papers in Education* 25, no. 3 (2010): 347.
7. Jeanette Elwood, "Assessment and Children's Rights," presentation to the meeting of the Formative Assessment for Students and Teachers State Collaborative, Phoenix, Arizona, 8 October 2011.
8. Elwood and Lundy, "Revisioning," 349.
9. Association of Professionals in Education and Children's Trusts (Aspect), "Personalised Learning: From Blueprint to Practice," http://www.aspect.org.uk/files/1188/PL%20From%20Blueprint%20to%20Practice.pdf.
10. Philip H. Winne and Nancy E. Perry, "Measuring Self-Regulated Learning," in *Handbook of Self-Regulation,* ed. Monique Boekaerts, Paul R. Pintrich, and Moshe Zeidner (San Diego, CA: Elsevier Academic Press, 2000), 531–566; Barry J. Zimmerman, "Self-Regulated Learning

and Academic Achievement: An Overview," *Educational Psychologist* 25, no. 1 (1990): 3–17; Monique Boekaerts and Lyn Corno, "Self-Regulation in the Classroom: A Perspective on Assessment and Intervention," *Applied Psychology: An International Review* 54, no. 2 (2005): 199–231.

11. Monique Boekaerts, "Motivated Learning: The Study of Student Situational Transactional Units," *European Journal of Psychology of Education* 14, no. 4 (1999): 41–55.

12. Linda Allal, "Assessment and the Regulation of Learning," in *International Encyclopedia of Education*, 3rd. ed., eds. Penelope Peterson, Eva Baker, and Barry McGaw (Oxford, UK: Elsevier, 2010), 349.

13. Frederick Erickson, "Some Thoughts on 'Proximal' Formative Assessment of Student Learning," *Yearbook of the National Society for the Study of Education* 106, no. 1 (2007): 187.

14. Lorrie A. Shepard, "Linking Formative Assessment to Scaffolding," *Educational Leadership* 63, no. 3 (2005): 66–71.

15. D. Royce Sadler, "Formative Assessment and the Design of Instructional Systems," *Instructional Science* 18, no. 2 (1989): 119–44.

16. James W. Pellegrino and Robert Glaser, "Analyzing Aptitudes for Learning: Inductive Reasoning," in *Advances in Instructional Psychology*, Vol. 2, ed. Robert Glaser (Hillsdale, NJ: Erlbaum, 1982), 325.

17. Black and Wiliam, "Assessment and Classroom Learning"; Paul J. Black et al., *Assessment for Learning: Putting It Into Practice* (New York: Open University Press, 2003); John Hattie and Helen Timperley, "The Power of Feedback," *Review of Educational Research* 77, no. 1 (2007): 81–112.

18. Paul J. Black, Mark Wilson, and Shih-Ying Yao, "Road Maps for Learning: A Guide to the Navigation of Learning Progressions," *Measurement: Interdisciplinary Research and Perspectives* 9, no. 2–3 (2011): 71–123.

19. Margaret Heritage, *Formative Assessment: Making It Happen In the Classroom* (Thousand Oaks, CA: Corwin Press, 2010); Harry Torrance and John Pryor, *Investigating Formative Assessment: Teaching, Learning, and Assessment in the Classroom* (Buckingham, UK: Open University Press, 1998); Linda Allal and Greta Pelgrims Ducrey, "Assessment of—or *in*—the Zone of Proximal Development," *Learning and Instruction* 10, no. 2 (2000): 137–52.

20. Lev S. Vygotsky, *Thought and Language* (Cambridge, MA: The MIT Press, 1986), 188.

21. Lev S. Vygotsky, *Mind and Society: The Development of Higher Mental Processes* (Cambridge, MA: Harvard University Press, 1978).

22. Ibid.

23. Barbara Rogoff and William Gardner, "Adult Guidance of Cognitive Development," in *Everyday Cognition: Development in Social Context*, ed. Barbara Rogoff and Jean Lave (Cambridge, MA: Harvard University Press, 1984), 95–116; James V. Wertsch, "From Social Interaction to Higher Psychological Processes: A Clarification and Application of Vygotsky's Theory," *Human Development* 22, no. 1 (1979): 1–22; David Wood, Jerome S. Bruner, and Gail Ross, "The Role of Tutoring in Problem Solving," *Journal of Child Psychology and Psychiatry* 17, (1976): 89–100.

24. Roland G. Tharp and Ronald Gallimore, *Rousing Minds to Life: Teaching, Learning, and Schooling in Social Context* (Cambridge, UK: Cambridge University Press, 1991).

25. Ann L. Brown and Robert A. Reeve, "Bandwidths of Competence: The Role of Supportive Contexts in Learning and Development," in *Development and Learning: Conflict or Congruence?*, ed. Lynn S. Liben (Hillsdale, NJ: Lawrence Erlbaum, 1987), 173–223.

26. Margaret Heritage and John Heritage, "Teacher Questioning: The Epicenter of Instruction and Assessment" [paper presented at the annual meeting of the American Educational Research Association, New Orleans, LA, April 2011].

27. Jean Lave and Etienne Wenger, *Situated Learning: Legitimate Peripheral Participation* (Cambridge, UK: Cambridge University Press, 1991); Gavriel Salomon, "No Distribution Without Individuals' Cognition: A Dynamic Interactional View," in *Distributed Cognitions: Psychological and Educational Considerations*, ed. Gavriel Salomon (Cambridge, UK: Cambridge University Press, 1993), 111–38.

28. E.g., National Research Council, *How People Learn: Brain, Mind, Experience, and School* (Washington, DC: National Academies Press, 2000); National Research Council, *Knowing What Students Know: The Science of Design and Educational Assessment* (Washington, DC: National Academies Press, 2001).

29. National Research Council, *How People Learn: Brain, Mind, Experience, and School* (Washington, DC: National Academies Press, 2000), 47; Deborah Jones, "Speaking, Listening, Planning, and Assessing: The Teacher's Role in Developing Metacognitive Awareness," *Early Child Development and Care* 177, no. 6–7 (2007): 571; Deanna Kuhn, "Metacognitive Development," *Current Directions in Psychological Science* 9, no. 5 (2000): 178.

30. Carl Bereiter and Marlene Scardamalia, "Intentional Learning as a Goal of Instruction," in *Knowing, Learning, and Instruction: Essays in Honor of Robert Glaser*, ed. Lauren B. Resnick (Hillsdale, NJ: Lawrence Erlbaum, 1989), 361–92.

31. Vygotsky, *Thought and Language.*

32. Kuhn, "Metacognitive Development," 178–81.

33. M. Suzanne Donovan and John D. Bransford, "Introduction," in *How Students Learn: History, Mathematics, and Science in the Classroom*, ed. M. Suzanne Donovan and John D. Bransford (Washington, DC: National Academies Press, 2005), 1–28; James W. Pellegrino, "Rethinking and Redesigning Curriculum, Instruction, and Assessment: What Contemporary Research and Theory Suggests" (Washington, DC: National Center for the New Commission on the Skills of the American Workforce, 2006).

34. Deborah Jones, "Speaking, Listening, Planning, and Assessing: The Teacher's Role in Developing Metacognitive Awareness," *Early Child Development and Care* 177, no. 6–7 (2007): 596–76.

35. Black and Wiliam, "Assessment and Classroom Learning."

Chapter 1

1. Etienne Wenger, *Communities of Practice: Learning, Meaning, and Identity* (New York: Cambridge University Press, 1998).

2. Ibid.

3. Jean Lave, *Cognition in Practice: Mind, Mathematics and Culture in Everyday Life* (New York: Cambridge University Press, 1988).

4. Wenger, *Communities of Practice*.

5. Jerome S. Bruner, *The Culture of Education* (Cambridge, MA: Harvard University Press, 1996).

6. John Seely Brown and Paul Duguid, "Knowledge and Organization: A Social-Practice Perspective," *Organization Science* 12, no. 2 (2001): 198–213.

7. James G. Greeno and the Middle School Mathematics Through Application Project Group, "The Situativity of Knowing, Learning, and Research," *American Psychologist* 53, no. 1 (1998): 5–26.

8. John Dewey, *The Child and the Curriculum* (Chicago, IL: University of Chicago Press, 1990), 208–209.

9. Linda Allal, "Situated Cognition and Learning: From Conceptual Frameworks to Classroom Investigations," *Revue Suisse des Sciences de l'Education* 23, no. 3 (2001): 407–22.

10. James G. Greeno, Allan M. Collins, and Lauren B. Resnick, "Cognition and Learning," in *Handbook of Educational Psychology,* ed. David C. Berliner and Robert C. Calfee (New York: Macmillan, 1996), 15–46.

11. John Seely Brown, Allan M. Collins, and Paul Duguid, "Situated Cognition and the Culture of Learning," *Educational Researcher* 18, no. 1 (1989): 32–42.

12. Allan M. Collins, John Seely Brown, and Susan E. Newman, "Cognitive Apprenticeship: Teaching the Craft of Reading, Writing, and Mathematics," in *Knowing, Learning, and Instruction: Essays in Honor of Robert Glaser,* ed. Lauren B. Resnick (Hillsdale, NJ: Lawrence Erlbaum, 1989), 453–94.

13. Greeno, Collins, and Resnick, "Cognition and Learning," 15–46.

14. Lee S. Shulman, "Signature Pedagogies in the Professions," *Daedalus* 134, no. 3 (2005): 52–59.

15. Ibid., 52.

16. Learning and Skills Improvement Service (LSIS), "Assessment for Learning," National STEM Centre, 2000-2009, accessed May 1, 2012. http://www.nationalstemcentre.org.uk/elibrary/resource/2424/assessment-for-learning.

17. Description adapted from the video http://www.successatthecore.com/teacher_development_featured_video.aspx?v=38.

18. Adapted from E. Caroline Wylie, "Formative Assessment: Why We Need It and How We Can Create the Condition That Will Allow It to Thrive" (presentation to the ETS Research Forum, Washington, DC, December 13, 2011).

19. Melissa S. Gresalif, "Taking Up Opportunities to Learn: Examining the Construction of Participatory Mathematical Identities in Middle School Classrooms." PhD diss., Stanford University, 2004.

20. cf. Collins, Brown, and Newman, "Cognitive Apprenticeship," 453–94.

21. D. Royce Sadler, "Formative Assessment and the Design of Instructional Systems," *Instructional Science* 18 (1989): 119–144.

22. Rogers Hall and Andee Rubin, "There's Five Little Notches in Here: Dilemmas in Teaching and Learning the Conventional Structure of Rate," in *Thinking Practices in Mathematics and Science Learning,* ed. James G. Greeno and Shelley V. Goldman (Mahwah, NJ: Lawrence Erlbaum, 1998), 189–236.

23. Melissa Gresalfi et al., "Constructing Competence: An Analysis of Student Participation in the Activity Systems of Mathematics Classrooms," *Educational Studies in Mathematics* 70 (2009): 49–70.

24. Paul J. Black, Mark Wilson, and Shih-Ying Yao, "Road Maps for Learning: A Guide to the Navigation of Learning Progressions," *Measurement: Interdisciplinary Research and Perspectives* 9, no. 2–3 (2011): 98.

25. Ted R. Sizer and Nancy F. Sizer, *The Students Are Watching: Schools and the Moral Contract.* (Boston, MA: Beacon Press, 1999), xvii.

26. Gloria Ladson-Billings, *The Dreamkeepers: Successful Teachers of African American Children* (San Francisco, CA: Jossey-Bass, 1994).

27. cf. Magdalene Lampert, *Teaching Problems and the Problems of Teaching* (New Haven, CT: Yale University Press, 2001).

28. Carl R. Rogers, *A Way of Being* (Boston, MA: Houghton Mifflin, 1980), 143.

29. E.g., Deborah Schifter, "Learning to See the Invisible: What Skills and Knowledge Are Needed to Engage with Students' Mathematical Ideas?" in *Beyond Classical Pedagogy: Teaching Elementary School Mathematics,* ed. Terry Wood, Barbara S. Nelson, and Janet E. Warfield (Mahwah, NJ: Lawrence Erlbaum, 2001), 109–134.

30. Olivia Lozano [Para Los Niños Charter School, Los Angeles], in discussion with the author, June 15, 2010.

31. Harry Torrance and John Pryor, "Developing Formative Assessment in the Classroom: Using Action Research to Explore and Modify Theory," *British Educational Research Journal* 27, no. 5 (2001): 616.

32. Margaret Heritage, *Formative Assessment: Making It Happen In the Classroom* (Thousand Oaks, CA: Corwin Press, 2010).

33. Margaret Heritage, "Gathering Evidence of Student Understanding," in *SAGE Handbook of Research on Classroom Assessment,* ed. James H. McMillan (Thousand Oaks, CA: SAGE Publications, 2012), 179–95.

34. Lee S. Shulman, "Knowledge and Teaching: Foundations of the New Reform," *Harvard Educational Review* 57, no. 1 (1987): 1–22.

35. Courtney B. Cazden, *Classroom Discourse: The Language of Teaching and Learning* (Portsmouth, NH: Heinemann, 1988); Hugh Mehan, *Learning Lessons: Social Organization in the Classroom* (Cambridge, MA: Harvard University Press, 1979); John M. Sinclair and R. Malcolm Coulthard, *Towards an Analysis of Discourse: The English Used by Teachers and Pupils* (London, UK: Oxford University Press, 1975).

36. Heritage, *Formative Assessment,* 4.

37. Jannette Elwood and Laura Lundy, "Revisioning Assessment through a Children's Rights Approach: Implications for Policy, Process and Practice," *Research Papers in Education* 25, no. 3 (2010): 335–53.

38. Carol S. Dweck, "Mind-Sets and Equitable Education," *Principal Leadership* 10, no. 5 (2010): 26–29; Carol S. Dweck, *Self-Theories: Their Role in Motivation, Personality and Development* (Philadelphia, PA: Psychology Press, 1999).

Chapter 2

1. Paul J. Black and Dylan Wiliam, "Assessment and Classroom Learning," *Assessment in Education: Principles Policy and Practice* 5 (1998): 37.

2. National Research Council, *Knowing What Students Know: The Science of Design and Educational Assessment* (Washington, DC: National Academies Press, 2001).

3. James W. Pellegrino, "Rethinking and Redesigning Curriculum, Instruction, and Assessment: What Contemporary Research and Theory Suggests" (Washington, DC: National Center for the New Commission on the Skills of the American Workforce, 2006), 3.

4. E.g., Alicia C. Alonzo and Maryl Gearhart, "Considering Learning Progressions from a Classroom Assessment Perspective," *Measurement* 14, no. 1 & 2 (2006): 99–104; Alicia C. Alonzo and Amelia W. Gotwals, eds., *Learning Progressions in Science: Current Challenges and Future Directions* (Rotterdam, Netherlands: Sense Publishers, 2012); Alison L. Bailey, Margaret Heritage, and Kimberly Reynolds Kelly, "The Dynamic Language Learning Project" (presentation to the World-Class Instructional Design and Assessment [WIDA] Assessment Consortium, Wisconsin Center for Education Research, Madison, WI, December 8, 2011); Jeffrey E. Barrett et al., "Evaluating and Improving a Learning Trajectory for Linear Measurement in Elementary Grades 2 and 3: A Longitudinal Study," *Mathematical Thinking and Learning* 14 (2012): 28–54; Paul J. Black, Mark Wilson, and Shih-Ying Yao, "Road Maps for Learning: A Guide to the Navigation of Learning Progressions," *Measurement: Interdisciplinary Research and Perspectives* 9, no. 2–3 (2011): 71–123; Jere Confrey, Alan P. Maloney, and Kenny H. Nguyen, *Learning Over Time: Learning Trajectories in Mathematics Education* (Charlotte, NC: Information Age Publishers, 2011); Tom Corcoran, Fritz A. Mosher, and Aaron Rogat, "Learning Progressions in Science: An Evidence-Based Approach to Reform of Teaching" (New York: Consortium for Policy Research in Education, 2009), 1–84; Cathleen A. Kennedy and Mark Wilson, "Using Progress Variables to Map Intellectual Development," in *Assessing and Modeling Cognitive Development in School,* ed. Robert W. Lissitz (Maple Grove, MN: JAM Press, 2007), 271–298; Nancy B. Songer, Ben Kelcey, and Amelia W. Gotwals, "How and When Does Complex Reasoning Occur? Empirically Driven Development of a Learning Progression Focused on Complex Reasoning About Biodiversity," *Journal for Research in Science Teaching* 46, no. 6 (2009): 610–31.

5. Kennedy and Wilson, "Using Progress Variables," 271–298; Geoff N. Masters and Margaret Forster, *Progress Maps: Assessment Resource Kit* (Camberwell, Australia: The Australian Council for Educational Research, 1996); Confrey et al., *Learning Over Time.*

6. Peter Lee and Rosalyn Ashby, "Progression in Historical Understanding among Students Ages 7-14," in *Knowing, Teaching, and Learning History: National and International Perspectives,* eds. Peter N. Stearns, Peter Seixas, and Sam Wineburg (New York: New York University Press, 2000), 199–222; Dylan Wiliam, "Keeping Learning on Track: Classroom Assessment and the Regulation of Learning," in *Second Handbook of Research on Mathematics Teaching and Learning,* ed. Frank K. Lester Jr. (Greenwich, CT: Information Age Publishing, 2007), 1053–98.

7. Frederic A. Mosher, *The Role of Learning Progressions in Standards-Based Education Reform* (Philadelphia, PA: Consortium for Policy Research in Education, Graduate School of Education, University of Pennsylvania, 2011), 2.

8. Corcoran et al., "Learning Progressions in Science," 37.

9. Songer, Kelcey, and Gotwals, "How and When Does Complex Reasoning Occur?," 612.

10. Masters and Forster, *Progress Maps,* 1.

11. Jere Confrey and Alan P. Maloney, "A Next Generation of Mathematics Assessments Based on Learning Trajectories" (paper presented at the conference Designing Technology—Enabled Diagnostic Assessments for K–12 Mathematics, Raleigh, NC, November 2010).

12. National Research Council, *Taking Science to School: Learning and Teaching Science in Grades K–8* (Washington, DC: National Academies Press, 2007), 219–20.

13. Ibid.

14. Barrett et al., "Evaluating and Improving a Learning Trajectory," 28–54; Richard J. Shavelson, Stanford Educational Assessment Laboratory (SEAL), and Curriculum Research and Development Group (CRDG), "Embedding Assessments in the FAST Curriculum: The Romance Between Curriculum and Assessment" (Final Report) (Palo Alto, CA: Stanford University, 2005).

15. M. Suzanne Donovan and John D. Bransford, "Introduction," in *How Students Learn: History, Mathematics, and Science in the Classroom,* eds. M. Suzanne Donovan and John D. Bransford (Washington, DC: National Academies Press, 2005), 1–28.

16. Jerome S. Bruner, *The Process of Education* (Cambridge, MA: Harvard University Press, 1960), 4.

17. Mosher, *The Role of Learning Progressions*, 1–16.

18. Laurel Hartley, personal communication to Charles W. Anderson, February 14, 2008, quoted in Charles W. Anderson, "Conceptual and Empirical Validation of Learning Progressions—Response to 'Learning Progressions: Supporting Instruction and Formative Assessment'" (presentation to the Consortium for Policy Research in Education Conference, Philadelphia, PA, February 2008).

19. Jere Confrey, "DELTA Professional Development Materials for Equipartitioning" (unpublished research materials; research assistance from P. Holt Wilson and C. Edgington, 2010).

20. Ibid.

21. Hollis S. Scarborough, "Connecting Early Language and Literacy to Later Reading (Dis)abilities: Evidence, Theory and Practice," in *Handbook of Early Literacy Research,* eds. Susan B. Neuman and David K. Dickinson (New York: Guilford Press, 2001), 97–110.

22. Mosher, *The Role of Learning Progressions*, 1–16; National Research Council, *Taking Science to School.*

23. Corcoran et al., "Learning Progressions in Science," 1–84.

24. John Dewey, *The Child and the Curriculum* (Chicago, IL: University of Chicago Press, 1902, repr., 1990), 198–99.

25. Mary A. White, "The View From the Pupil's Desk," *The Urban Review* 2, no. 5 (1968): 5–7.

26. Patrick Griffin, "The Comfort of Competence and the Uncertainty of Assessment," *Studies in Educational Evaluation* 33, (2007): 87–99.

27. National Research Council, *Taking Science to School.*

28. Barrett et al., "Evaluating and Improving a Learning Trajectory," 32.

29. Arizona Board of Regents, *Progressions Documents for the Common Core Math Standards,* last modified 2007, http://ime.math.arizona.edu/progressions/.

30. California State Board of Education, *California Health Standards,* last modified September 27, 2011, http://www.cde.ca.gov/be/st/ss/.

31. Arizona Board of Regents, *Progressions Documents.*

32. Laurel Hartley, personal communication to Charles W. Anderson, February 14, 2008, quoted in Charles W. Anderson, "Conceptual and Empirical Validation of Learning Progressions— Response to 'Learning Progressions: Supporting Instruction and Formative Assessment'" (presentation to the Consortium for Policy Research in Education Conference, Philadelphia, PA, February 2008).

33. Jason Riley, "Learning Progressions" (presentation to the National Student Assessment Conference, Detroit, MI, June 26, 2010).

Chapter 3

1. D. Royce Sadler, "Formative Assessment and the Design of Instructional Systems," *Instructional Science* 18 (1989): 119–44.

2. Frederick Erickson, personal communication to author, October 28, 2009.

3. John Dewey, "Progressive Education and the Science of Education," *Progressive Education* 5 (1928): 204.

4. Patrick Griffin, "The Comfort of Competence and the Uncertainty of Assessment," *Studies in Educational Evaluation* 33 (2007): 87–99.

5. Sadler, "Formative Assessment," 119–44.

6. Frederick Erickson, "Some Thoughts on 'Proximal' Formative Assessment of Student Learning," *Yearbook of the National Society for the Study of Education* 106, no. 1 (2007): 186–216.

7. Richard A. Lesh et al., "Principles for Developing Thought-Revealing Activities for Students and Teachers," in *Research Design in Mathematics and Science Education,* eds. Anthony E. Kelly and Richard A. Lesh (Mahwah, NJ: Lawrence Erlbaum, 2000), 591–646.

8. Margaret Heritage, "Gathering Evidence of Student Understanding," in *SAGE Handbook of Research on Classroom Assessment,* ed. James H. McMillan (Thousand Oaks, CA: SAGE Publications, 2012), 179–95.

9. Courtney B. Cazden, *Classroom Discourse: The Language of Teaching and Learning* (Portsmouth, NH: Heinemann, 1988); Hugh Mehan, *Learning Lessons: Social Organization in the Classroom* (Cambridge, MA: Harvard University Press, 1979); John M. Sinclair and R. Malcolm Coulthard, *Towards An Analysis of Discourse: The English Used By Teachers and Pupils* (London, UK: Oxford University Press, 1975).

10. Mary E. Webb and Jane Jones, "Exploring Tensions in Developing Assessment for Learning," *Assessment in Education: Principles, Policy & Practice* 16, no. 2 (2009): 165–84.

11. Maria A. Ruiz-Primo and Erin M. Furtak, "Informal Formative Assessment and Scientific Inquiry: Exploring Teachers' Practices and Student Learning," *Educational Assessment* 11, no. 3–4 (2006): 205–35.

12. Wynne Harlen, "Formative Classroom Assessment in Science and Mathematics," in *Formative Classroom Assessment: Theory into Practice,* ed. James H. McMillan (New York: Teachers College Press, 2007), 116–35.

13. Paul J. Black, Mark Wilson, and Shih-Ying Yao, "Road Maps for Learning: A Guide to the Navigation of Learning Progressions," *Measurement: Interdisciplinary Research and Perspectives* 9, no. 2–3 (2011): 71–123.

14. Jeffrey K. Smith, "Reconsidering Reliability in Classroom Assessment and Grading," *Educational Measurement: Issues and Practice* 22, no. 4 (2003): 30.

15. Heritage, "Gathering Evidence," 179–95.

16. Linda Allal, "Assessment and the Regulation of Learning," in *International Encyclopedia of Education*, 3rd ed., ed. Penelope Peterson, Eva Baker, and Barry McGaw (Oxford, UK: Elsevier, 2010), 348–52; Paul J. Black and Dylan Wiliam, "Developing the Theory of Formative Assessment," *Educational Assessment, Evaluation, and Accountability* 21, (2009): 5–31; Harlen, "Formative Classroom Assessment," 116-135; Margaret Heritage and John Heritage, "Teacher Questioning: The Epicenter of Instruction and Assessment" (paper presented at the annual meeting of the American Educational Research Association, New Orleans, LA, April 2011); Brigitte Jordan and Peter Putz, "Assessment as Practice: Notes on Measures, Tests, and Targets," *Human Organization* 63, no. 3 (2004): 346–58; Ruiz-Primo and Furtak, "Informal Formative Assessment and Scientific Inquiry," 205–35; Maria A. Ruiz-Primo and Erin M. Furtak, "Exploring Teachers' Informal Formative Assessment Practices and Students' Understanding in the Context of Scientific Inquiry," *Journal of Educational Research in Science Teaching* 44, no. 1 (2007): 57–84; Harry Torrance and John Pryor, *Investigating Formative Assessment: Teaching, Learning, and Assessment in the Classroom* (Buckingham, UK: Open University Press, 1998).

17. Paul J. Black and Dylan Wiliam, "A Pleasant Surprise," *Phi Delta Kappan* 92, no. 1 (2010): 47–48.

18. Linda Allal and Greta Pelgrims Ducrey, "Assessment of—or *in*—the Zone of Proximal Development," *Learning and Instruction* 10 (2000): 137–52; Lev S. Vygotsky, *Mind and Society: The Development of Higher Mental Processes* (Cambridge, MA: Harvard University Press, 1978).

19. Harry Torrance and John Pryor, "Developing Formative Assessment in the Classroom: Using Action Research to Explore and Modify Theory," *British Educational Research Journal* 27, no. 5 (2001): 615–31.

20. John Heritage and Geoffrey Raymond, "Navigating Epistemic Landscapes: Acquiescence, Agency and Resistance in Responses to Polar Questions," in *Questions: Formal, Functional and Interactional Perspectives,* ed. Jan P. de Ruiter (Cambridge, UK: Cambridge University Press, 2012), 179–92.

21. Paul J. Black and Dylan Wiliam, "Assessment and Classroom Learning," *Assessment in Education: Principles Policy and Practice* 5 (1998): 7–73.

22. Lorrie A. Shepard, "Will Commercialization Enable or Destroy Formative Assessment?" (Original Title: "Formative Assessment: Caveat Emptor") (paper presented at the ETS Invitational Conference 2005: The Future of Assessment, Shaping Teaching and Learning, New York, NY, October 2005).

23. Alison L. Bailey and Margaret Heritage, *Formative Assessment for Literacy, Grades K–6: Building Reading and Academic Language Skills Across the Curriculum* (Thousand Oaks, CA: Corwin/Sage Press, 2008).

24. Richard J. Shavelson, Stanford Educational Assessment Laboratory (SEAL), and Curriculum Research and Development Group (CRDG), "Embedding Assessments in the FAST Curriculum: The Romance Between Curriculum and Assessment" (Final Report) (Palo Alto, CA: Stanford University, 2005).

25. Kathi Cook, Cathy Seeley, and Linda Chaput, "Customizing and Capture: Online Assessment Tools for Secondary Mathematics," in *New Frontiers in Formative Assessment,* eds. Pendred E. Noyce and Daniel T. Hickey (Cambridge, MA: Harvard Education Press, 2011), 69–88.

26. Nicole Cohen et al., "Becoming Strategic Readers: Three Cases Using Formative Assessment, UDL, and Technology to Support Struggling Middle School Readers," in *New Frontiers in Formative Assessment,* eds. Pendred E. Noyce and Daniel T. Hickey (Cambridge, MA: Harvard Education Press, 2011), 129–40.

27. Dylan Wiliam, "What is Assessment for Learning?" *Studies in Educational Evaluation* 37 (2011): 3–14.

28. Ibid.

Chapter 4

1. Adapted from a teacher video used for professional development by the New York Comprehensive Center Formative Assessment Project, 2009.

2. D. Royce Sadler, "Formative Assessment and the Design of Instructional Strategies," *Instructional Science* 18 (1989): 119–44.

3. Alex Kozulin et al., eds., *Vygotsky's Educational Theory in Cultural Context* (Cambridge, UK: Cambridge University Press, 2003).

4. Roland G. Tharp and Ronald Gallimore, *Rousing Minds to Life* (Cambridge, UK: Cambridge University Press, 1988).

5. Lev S. Vygotsky, *Mind and Society: The Development of Higher Mental Processes* (Cambridge, MA: Harvard University Press, 1978), 87.

6. Jerome S. Bruner, *The Process of Education* (Cambridge, MA: Harvard University Press, 1960).

7. Aída Walqui and Margaret Heritage, "Instruction for Diverse Groups of English Language Learners," in *Understanding Language: Commissioned Papers on Language and Literacy Issues in the Common Core State Standards and Next Generation Science Standards,* eds. Kenji Hakuta and Maria Santos (Palo Alto, CA: Stanford University, 2012), 93–104.

8. Ann L. Brown and Robert A. Reeve, "Bandwidths of Competence: The Role of Supportive Contexts in Learning and Development," in *Development and Learning: Conflict or Congruence?,* ed. Lynn S. Liben (Hillsdale, NJ: Lawrence Erlbaum, 1987), 173–223.

9. Jim Minstrell, Ruth Anderson, and Min Li, "Assessing Teacher Competency in Formative Assessment," *Annual Report 2009* (Seattle, WA: FACET Innovations, 2009).

10. Jean Piaget, "Piaget's Theory," in *Carmichael's Manual of Child Psychology,* Vol. 1, ed. Paul H. Mussen (New York: John Wiley & Sons, 1970), 715.

11. Barbara Jones, "Learning Progressions and Formative Assessment," (presentation to the Arizona School Improvement Formative Assessment Workshop, Phoenix, AZ, 10 February 2012).

12. E.g., Pauline Gibbons, *Scaffolding Language, Scaffolding Learning: Teaching Second Language Learners in the Mainstream Classroom* (Portsmouth, NH: Heinemann, 2002).

13. David Wood, Jerome S. Bruner, and Gail Ross, "The Role of Tutoring in Problem Solving," *Journal of Child Psychology and Psychiatry* 17 (1976): 89–100.

14. Janneke van de Pol, Monique Volman, and Jos Beishuizen, "Scaffolding in Teacher-Student Interaction: A Decade of Research," *Educational Psychology Review* 22, no. 3 (2010): 271–96.

15. Janet E. Spector, "Predicting Progress in Beginning Reading: Dynamic Assessment of Awareness," *Journal of Educational Psychology* 84, no. 3 (1992): 353–63.

16. Robert E. Slavin, "Educational Psychology: Theory and Practice." 2010, http://wps.ablongman.com/ab_slavin_edpsych_8/38/9951/2547615.cw/index.htm.

17. C. Addison Stone, "The Metaphor of Scaffolding: Its Utility for the Field of Learning Disabilities," *Journal of Learning Disabilities* 31, no. 4 (1998): 344–64.

18. Tharp and Gallimore, *Rousing Minds to Life.*

19. Ibid., 63.

20. Gene Lerner, "Collaborative Turn Sequences," in *Conversation Analysis: Studies From the First Generation,* ed. Gene Lerner (Amsterdam, Netherlands: John Benjamins, 2004), 225–56.

21. E.g., Ruth Butler, "Task-involving and Ego-involving Properties of Evaluation: Effects of Different Feedback Conditions on Motivational Perceptions, Interest, and Performance," *Journal of Educational Psychology* 79, no. 4 (1987): 474–82; Robert L. Bangert-Drowns et al., "The Instructional Effect of Feedback in Test-like Events," *Review of Educational Research* 61, no. 2 (1991): 213–38; Avraham N. Kluger and Angelo DeNisi, "The Effects of Feedback Interventions on Performance: A Historical Review, a Meta-analysis, and a Preliminary Feedback Intervention Theory," *Psychological Bulletin* 119, no. 2 (1996): 254–84; Edna Holland Mory, "Feedback Research Revisited," in *Handbook of Research on Educational Communications and Technology,* ed. David H. Jonassen (Mahwah, NJ: Lawrence Erlbaum, 2004), 745–83.

22. Valerie J. Shute, "Focus on Formative Feedback," Educational Testing Service Research Report No. RR-07-01 (Princeton, NJ: Educational Testing Service, 2007).

23. Kluger and DeNisi, "The Effects of Feedback Interventions," 254–84.

24. E.g., Anastasiya A. Lipnevich and Jeffrey K. Smith, "Response to Assessment Feedback: The Effects of Grades, Praise, and Source of Information" (Washington, DC: ETS Research Forum, 2008); John Hattie and Helen Timperley, "The Power of Feedback," *Review of Educational Research* 77, no. 1 (2007): 81–112; Shute, "Focus on Formative Feedback."

25. Raymond Kulhavy and William A. Stock, "Feedback in Written Instruction: The Place of Response Certitude," *Educational Psychology Review* 1, no. 4 (1989): 279–308.

26. Adapted from the video http://www.edugains.ca/newsite/aer2/aervideo/descriptivefeedback.html.

27. Suffolk County Council, "'How Am I Doing?'—Assessment and Feedback to Learners" (Ipswich, UK: Suffolk Advisory Service, 2001). Accessed August 13, 2012. http://www.hvlc.org.uk/ace/aifl/docs/B1/How_am_I_doing.pdf.

28. Ibid.

29. Adapted from International Reading Association/National Council of Teachers of English. "Reciprocal Revision: Making Peer Feedback Meaningful." Accessed July 9, 2012. http://www.readwritethink.org/classroom-resources/lesson-plans/reciprocal-revision-making-peer-403.html.

30. Shirley Clarke, *Targeting Assessment in the Primary Classroom: Strategies for Planning, Assessment, Pupil Feedback and Target Setting* (London, UK: Hodder Murray, 1998).

31. Ibid., 72.

32. Bangert-Drowns et al., "The Instructional Effect of Feedback," 213–38.

33. John Threlfall, "The Formative Use of Assessment Information in Planning—The Notion of Contingent Planning," *British Journal of Educational Studies* 53, no. 1 (2005): 54–65.

34. Minstrell et al., "Assessing Teacher Competency."

35. Paul J. Black and Dylan Wiliam, "Developing the Theory of Formative Assessment," *Educational Assessment, Evaluation, and Accountability* 21, no. 1 (2009): 10.

36. Walqui and Heritage, "Instruction for Diverse Groups of English Language Learners," 93–104.

Chapter 5

1. Mary James et al., *Learning How to Learn: Tools for Schools* (New York: Routledge, 2006).

2. Seymour Papert, "Child Power: Keys to the New Learning of the Digital Century" (speech delivered at the Eleventh Colin Cherry Memorial Lecture on Communication, Imperial College, London, UK, June 2, 1998).

3. Paul J. Black et al., "Learning How to Learn and Assessment for Learning: A Theoretical Inquiry," *Research Papers in Education* 21, no. 2 (2006): 119–32.

4. Steve Higgins et al., "Learning to Learn in Schools Phase 3 Evaluation Year One Final Report" (London, UK: Campaign for Learning, 2005); Steve Higgins et al., "Learning to Learn in Schools Phase 3 Evaluation Year Two Final Report" (London, UK: Campaign for Learning, 2006); Steve Higgins et al., "Learning to Learn in Schools Phase 3 Evaluation Final Report" (London, UK: Campaign for Learning, 2007).

5. David H. Hargreaves, *Personalising Learning, 3: Learning to Learn and the New Technologies* (London, UK: Specialist Schools and Academies Trust, 2005).

6. Black et al. "Learning How to Learn," 120.

7. Margaret Heritage, *Formative Assessment: Making It Happen In the Classroom* (Thousand Oaks, CA: Corwin Press, 2010).

8. Ibid., 4.

9. Deborah Jones, "Speaking, Listening, Planning, and Assessing: The Teacher's Role in Developing Metacognitive Awareness," *Early Child Development and Care* 177, no. 6–7 (2007): 571; Deanna Kuhn, "Metacognitive Development," *Current Directions in Psychological Science* 9, no. 5 (2000): 178; National Research Council, *How People Learn: Brain, Mind, Experience, and School* (Washington, DC: National Academies Press, 2000), 97.

10. M. Suzanne Donovan and John D. Bransford, eds., *How Students Learn: History, Mathematics, and Science in the Classroom* (Washington, DC: National Academies Press, 2005); Lev S. Vygotsky, *Thought and Language* (Cambridge, MA: The MIT Press, 1962).

11. E.g., Ann L. Brown, "Metacognition: The Development of Selective Attention Strategies for Learning from Texts," in *Directions in Reading: Research and Instruction (Thirtieth Yearbook of the National Reading Conference),* ed. Michael L. Kamil (Washington, DC: The National Reading Conference, 1981); Gary D. Phye, "Inductive Reasoning and Problem Solving: The Early Grades," in *Handbook of Academic Learning: Construction of Knowledge,* ed. Gary D. Phye (San Diego, CA: Academic Press, 1997), 452–73; Barry J. Zimmerman and Dale H. Schunk, *Handbook of Self-Regulation of Learning and Performance* (New York: Routledge, 2011).

12. Carl Bereiter and Marlene Scardamalia, "Intentional Learning as a Goal of Instruction," in *Knowing, Learning, and Instruction: Essays in Honor of Robert Glaser,* ed. Lauren B. Resnick (Hillsdale, NJ: Lawrence Erlbaum, 1989), 361–92.

13. Dale H. Schunk, "Modeling and Attributional Effects on Children's Achievement: A Self-Efficacy Analysis," *Journal of Educational Psychology* 73, (1981): 93–105; Dale H. Schunk, "Self-Efficacy Perspective on Achievement Behavior," *Educational Psychologist* 19 (1984): 48–58; Barry J. Zimmerman and Manuel Martinez-Pons, "Development of a Structured Interview for Assessing Student Use of Self-Regulated Learning Strategies," *American Educational Research Journal* 23, no. 4 (1986): 614–28; Barry J. Zimmerman and Manuel Martinez-Pons, "Construct Validation of a Strategy Model of Student Self-Regulated Learning," *Journal of Educational Psychology* 80, no. 3 (1988): 284–90.

14. Mary A. White, "The View From the Pupil's Desk," *The Urban Review* 2, no. 5 (1968): 6.

15. Bereiter and Scardamalia, "Intentional Learning as a Goal," 361–92.

16. White, "The View," 7.

17. The Inquiry Project: Bridging Research & Practice. "Goals for Productive Discussions and Nine Talk Moves." Accessed July 13, 2012. http://inquiryproject.terc.edu/shared/pd/Goals_and_Moves.pdf; Suzanne H. Chapin, Catherine O'Connor, and Nancy C. Anderson, *Classroom Discussions: Using Math Talk to Help Students Learn, Grades 1-6* (Sausalito, CA: Math Solutions Publication, 2009).

18. cf. Marlene Scardamalia, Carl Bereiter, and Rosanne Steinbach, "Teachability of Reflective Processes in Written Composition," *Cognitive Science* 8 (1984): 173–90.

19. John Hattie and Helen Timperley, "The Power of Feedback," *Review of Educational Research* 77, no. 1 (2007): 86.

20. Hattie and Timperley, "The Power of Feedback," 90.

21. Jeanne D. Day and Luis A. Cordón, "Static and Dynamic Measures of Ability: An Experimental Comparison," *Journal of Educational Psychology* 85, no. 1 (1993): 75–82.

22. Robert L. Bangert-Drowns et al., "The Instructional Effect of Feedback in Test-like Events," *Review of Educational Research* 61, no. 2 (1991): 213–38.

23. National Research Council, *How People Learn.*

24. Barbara Y. White and John R. Frederiksen, "Inquiry, Modeling, and Metacognition: Making Science Accessible to All Students," *Cognition and Instruction* 16, no. 1 (1998): 3–118.

25. Eric Livingston, *Ethnographies of Reason* (Burlington, VT: Ashgate, 2008).

26. National Research Council, *How People Learn.*

27. Carol S. Dweck, "Mind-Sets and Equitable Education," *Principal Leadership* 10, no. 5 (2010): 26–29; Robert L. Bangert-Drowns et al., "The Instructional Effect," 213–38.

28. Carol S. Dweck, *Self-Theories: Their Role in Motivation, Personality and Development* (Philadelphia, PA: Psychology Press, 1999).

29. E.g., David Boud, Ruth Cohen, and Jane Sampson, "Peer Learning and Assessment," *Assessment and Evaluation in Higher Education* 24, no. 4 (1999): 413–26; Graham Gibbs, "Using Assessment Strategically to Change the Way Students Learn," in *Assessment Matters in Higher Education: Choosing and Using Diverse Approaches,* eds. Sally A. Brown and Angela Glasner (Buckingham, UK: Open University Press, 1999), 41–54.

30. Paul J. Black et al., *Assessment for Learning: Putting It Into Practice* (New York, NY: Open University Press, 2003).

31. Paul J. Black and Dylan Wiliam, "Assessment and Classroom Learning," *Assessment in Education: Principles Policy and Practice* 5, (1998): 7–73.

Chapter 6

1. Lorrie A. Shepard, "Will Commercialization Enable or Destroy Formative Assessment?" (Original Title: "Formative Assessment: Caveat Emptor") (paper presented at the ETS Invitational Conference 2005, New York, NY, October 2005), 2.

2. William Schmidt, Richard Houang, and Leland Cogan, "A Coherent Curriculum" *American Educator* (2002): 10-48.

3. Lorrie A. Shepard, "Classroom Assessment," in *Education Measurement*, 4th ed., ed. Robert L. Brennan (Westport, CT: Greenwood Publishing Group, 2006), 623–46.

4. Henry Braun, "Reconsidering the Impact of High-Stakes Testing," *Education Policy Analysis Archives* 12, no. 1 (2004): 1–43; Eric A. Hanushek and Margaret E. Raymond, "Does School Accountability Lead to Improved Student Performance?" *Journal of Policy Analysis and Management* 24, no. 2 (2005): 297–327; Barak Rosenshine, "High-Stakes Testing: Another Analysis," *Education Policy Analysis Archives* 11, no. 24 (2003): 1–8; National Research Council, *Incentives and Test-Based Accountability in Education* (Washington, DC: National Academies Press, 2011).

5. National Research Council, *Incentives and Test-Based Accountability.*

6. Paul J. Black and Dylan Wiliam, "Lessons from Around the World: How Policies, Politics and Cultures Constrain and Afford Assessment Practices," *Curriculum Journal* 16, no. 2 (2005): 260.

7. Jonathan Supovitz, "Can High Stakes Testing Leverage Educational Improvement? Prospects from the Last Decade of Testing and Accountability Reform," *Journal of Educational Change* 10, no. 2–3 (2009): 211–27.

8. Organisation for Economic Co-operation and Development (OECD), *Formative Assessment: Improving Learning in Secondary Classrooms* (Paris, France: OECD Publishing/Centre for Educational Research and Innovation, 2005); Sarah McManus, "Formative Assessment in North Carolina" (presentation to the Council of Chief State School Officers National Conference on Student Assessment, Minneapolis, MN, June 2012); Colleen Anderson, "Formative Assessment in Iowa" (presentation to the Council of Chief State School Officers Formative Assessment for Students and Teachers State Collaborative, Phoenix, AZ, November 2011); Ed Roeber, "Formative Assessment for Michigan Educators" (presentation to the Council of Chief State School Officers National Conference on Student Assessment, Minneapolis, MN, June 2012); Ian Clark, "Formative Assessment: Policy, Perspectives and Practice," *Florida Journal of Educational Administration and Policy* 4, no. 2 (2011): 158–80; Margaret Heritage, "Formative Assessment and Next-Generation Assessment Systems: Are We Losing An Opportunity?" (Washington, DC: Council of Chief State School Officers, 2010).

9. E.g., OECD, *Formative Assessment.*

10. OECD, *Education Policy Analysis: Focus on Higher Education 2005–2006* (Paris, France: OECD Publishing, 2006).

11. Ibid., 125.

12. Ibid., 131.

13. Department for Children, Families and Schools, "The Assessment for Learning Strategy" (Nottingham, UK: DCSF Publications, 2008), 10.

14. Carolyn Hutchinson and Louise Hayward, "The Journey So Far: Assessment for Learning in Scotland," *Curriculum Journal* 16, no. 2 (2005): 225–48.

15. Ibid.

16. OECD, *Education Policy Analysis.*

17. David Carless, *From Testing to Productive Student Learning: Implementing Formative Assessment in Confucian-Heritage Settings* (New York: Routledge, 2011), 83.

18. Ibid., 89.

19. OECD, *Education Policy Analysis*, 136.

20. National Research Council, *Incentives and Test-Based Accountability.*

21. Margaret Heritage, "Gathering Evidence of Student Understanding," in *SAGE Handbook of Research on Classroom Assessment*, ed. James H. McMillan (Thousand Oaks, CA: SAGE Publications, 2012), 179–95.

22. Heritage, "Formative Assessment and Next-Generation Assessment Systems."

23. Robert Rothman, "Principles for a Comprehensive Assessment System" (Washington, DC: Alliance for Excellent Education, 2010), 4.

24. Heritage, "Formative Assessment and Next-Generation Assessment Systems."

25. OECD, *Education Policy Analysis*, 122.

26. Western and Northern Canadian Protocol for Collaboration in Education (WNCP), "Rethinking Classroom Assessment with Purpose in Mind: Assessment for Learning, Assessment as Learning, Assessment of Learning" (Winnipeg, MB: Manitoba Education, Citizenship and Youth, 2006), 42.

27. The Ontario Ministry of Education, "Growing Success: Assessment, Evaluation, and Reporting in Ontario Schools (First Edition, Covering Grades 1 to 12)" (Toronto, ON: Queen's Printer for Ontario, 2010), 28.

28. Assessment as Part of Learning and Teaching, Education Scotland, retrieved August 14, 2012, from http://www.educationscotland.gov.uk/learningteachingandassessment/assessment/progressandachievement/howweassess/learningteachingandassessment/introduction.asp.

29. Carless, *From Testing to Productive*, 83.

30. OECD, *Education Policy Analysis.*

31. Deborah Nusche et al., "OECD Reviews of Evaluation and Assessment in Education: Norway" (Paris, France: OECD Publishing, 2011), 70.

32. Deborah Nusche et al., "OECD Reviews of Evaluation and Assessment in Education: Sweden" (Paris, France: OECD Publishing, 2011).

33. The New Zealand Ministry of Education, "OECD Review on Evaluation and Assessment Frameworks for Improving School Outcomes: New Zealand Country Background Report 2010" (Paris, France: OECD Publishing, 2010).

34. The Scottish Government, *Curriculum for Excellence: Building the Curriculum 5: A Framework for Assessment* (Edinburgh, UK: The Scottish Government, 2010), 23.

35. Janet W. Looney, "Integrating Formative and Summative Assessment: Progress Toward a Seamless System?" (OECD Education working paper no. 58, OECD Publishing, 2011), 13. Accessed August 10, 2012. doi: 10.1787/5kghx3kbl734-en.

36. The New Zealand Ministry of Education, *The New Zealand Curriculum: Mathematics Standards for Years 1-8* (Wellington, New Zealand: Learning Media Limited, 2009), 12.

37. Nusche et al., "OECD . . . Norway," 43.

38. Nusche et al., "OECD . . . Sweden," 8.

39. Ibid., 8; Rick Stiggins, "New Assessment Beliefs for a New School Mission," *Phi Delta Kappan* 86, no. 1 (2004): 22–27; "A Comprehensive Balanced Assessment System," Public Schools of North Carolina, retrieved August 14, 2012, from http://www.ncpublicschools.org/accountability/educators/vision/; "Professional Development Toolkit: Balanced Assessment," Virginia Department of Education, retrieved August 14, 2012, from http://www.doe.virginia.gov/teaching/career_resources/prof_dev_toolkit/balanced_assessment/.

40. http://nces.ed.gov/nationsreportcard/about/assessmentsched.asp.

41. National Assessment Program (NAP), Australian Curriculum Assessment and Reporting Authority (ACARA), retrieved August 14, 2012, from http://www.nap.edu.au/.

42. Nusche et al., "OECD . . . Norway," 25.

43. Ibid., 32.

44. Black and Wiliam, "Lessons from Around the World," 253.

45. Ibid.

46. Ibid.

47. Ibid., 249–61.

48. Terry J. Crooks, "Educational Assessment in New Zealand Schools," *Assessment in Education* 9, no. 2 (2002): 237–53; "The Benefits of Moderation—For Teachers," The New Zealand Ministry of Education, retrieved August 14, 2012, from http://assessment.tki.org.nz/Moderation/Moderation-professional-learning-modules/What-is-moderation/Benefits/The-benefits-of-moderation-for-teachers.

49. Valentina Klenowski and Claire Wyatt-Smith, "Standards, Teacher Judgment and Moderation in Contexts of National Curriculum and Assessment Reform," *Assessment Matters 2,* (2010): 115.

50. Black and Wiliam, "Lessons from Around the World," 251.

51. Heritage, "Formative Assessment and Next-Generation Assessment Systems."

52. http://www.smarterbalanced.org/smarter-balanced-assessments/

53. Lev S. Vygotsky, *Mind and Society: The Development of Higher Mental Processes.* (Cambridge, MA: Harvard University Press, 1978).

54. "Race to the Top Assessment Program," U.S. Department of Education, last modified May 25, 2012, http://www2.ed.gov/programs/racetothetop-assessment/index.html.

55. Judith Arter, "Interim Benchmark Assessments: Are We Getting Our Eggs in the Right Basket?" (paper presented at the National Council on Measurement in Education, Denver, CO, May 1, 2010).

56. OECD, *Education Policy Analysis*, 136.

57. Linda Darling-Hammond et al., "Professional Learning in the Learning Profession: A Status Report on Teacher Development in the United States and Abroad" (Dallas, TX: National Staff Development Council, 2009).

58. Jannette Elwood and Laura Lundy, "Revisioning Assessment Through a Children's Rights Approach: Implications for Policy, Process and Practice," *Research Papers in Education* 25, no. 3 (2010): 335–53.

59. Ibid., 347.

Acknowledgments

I owe a debt of gratitude to many people. I want to thank Jim Popham for encouraging me to write this book. Without his encouragement, in the summer of 2011, this book would not have been written. I am also delighted that Jim has written the foreword to the book.

I extend my gratitude to the participants in the International Network on Assessment for Learning meeting in Bergen, Norway, in June 2011 for pushing my thinking about formative assessment. I have a special word of thanks to Jannette Elwood for introducing me at this meeting to the ideas about a children's rights approach to assessment, which frame the chapters of this book.

My appreciative thanks go to all the teachers who are represented throughout the book and who have helped me learn about formative assessment from the work they do everyday with their students. Each one is remarkable.

I am indebted to my co-author for chapter 6, E. Caroline Wylie. Not only did she collaborate in hatching the ideas for this chapter and committing them to print, she has provided extremely useful feedback on each of the book's chapters.

At Harvard Education Press, I thank Caroline Chauncey for her prompt reviews of each chapter and for her tremendously helpful feedback. The book is truly a better one for all the time and thought she committed to the reviewing process.

I am especially grateful to Katelyn Lee for her invaluable assistance in the preparation of the manuscript.

Finally, I thank John Heritage. He knows this book and his support and contribution hold a very special meaning for me.

About the Author

Margaret Heritage is the assistant director for professional development at the National Center for Research on Evaluation, Standards, and Student Testing (CRESST) at the University of California, Los Angeles. Her current work focuses on formative assessment, including teachers' use of formative assessment evidence, and on the development and assessment of academic language for English language learners. She has published extensively and made numerous presentations on these topics all over the United States, and in Europe, Australia, and Asia.

Prior to joining CRESST, she taught in and held leadership positions at schools in the United Kingdom, including a period as a county inspector of education, and in the United States, where she was principal of the laboratory school of the Graduate School of Education and Information Studies at UCLA. At the higher education level, she has taught graduate classes at the department of education at the University of Warwick, United Kingdom, the University of California, Los Angeles, and at Stanford University.

Index